A H
Vaiṣṇava Songs and Practices

Compiled and edited by

Rāmānujāchārya Dās

INTERNATIONAL SOCIETY
FOR KRISHNA CONSCIOUSNESS
Founder-Ācārya His Divine Grace A. C.
Bhaktivedanta Swami Prabhupāda

Second Edition 2006
ISBN 81-87812-34-6
Published by: Rasbihari Lal & Sons.
Loi Bazar, Vrindaban-281121
(U.P.) India.
Phone: 91-565-2442570
Web: www.rasbiharilal.com
E-mail: brijwasi2001@hotmail.com

Our Other Publications

Dedicated to

His Divine Grace
A.C. Bhaktivedanta Swami Prabhupāda

"He lives forever by his divine instructions and the follower lives with him."

Contents

*All songs with an asterisk are in the Bengali language; all others are in Sanskrit, with the exception of the *Prema-dhvani* which is a mixture of Sanskrit, Bengali and Hindi.

Index of First Lines

Preface

By the mercy of the Supreme Personality of Godhead Śrī Kṛṣṇa and His devotees I have been intrumental in compiling and editing this *Handbook of Vaiṣṇava Songs and Practices.* It is specifically presented for persons who are now engaged in serving His Divine Grace A.C. Bhaktivedanta Swami Prabhupāda. I hope they will find it useful.

While compiling this handbook I have consulted Śrīla Prabhupāda's books and writings, and other publications of the Bhaktivedanta Book Trust, such as the *Songs of the Vaiṣṇava Ācāryas* and the *Pañcarātra Pradīpa* compiled by the GBC Deity Worship Research Group.

As you can see by examining the table of contents, there are two main parts of this handbook: "Vaiṣṇava Songs and Prayers" and "Vaiṣṇava Practices." The first part includes all of the main songs and prayers which are used for daily worship in our temples and homes. Also included are several popular *bhajans.* The second part includes the most important Vaiṣṇava devotional practices.

A special feature of this handbook is the inclusion of word meanings for all of the songs,, prayers and *mantras* in addition to their translations. By consulting these word meanings and translations one can more easily enter into an understanding of the original texts. Also included at the end of the table of contents is an "Index of First Lines" so that devotees can easily find the songs, prayers and *mantras* they are looking for. There is also a "Sanskrit and Bengali Pronunciation Guide" at the end of the handbook. This handbook has been produced in a handy pocket size so that the devotees can easily carry it with them, and consult and study it wherever they go.

I beg to offer my sincere thanks to all of the devotees who have helped me in the production of this handbook by giving me their support, encouragement and valuable suggestions. I would especially like to thank His Holiness Jaya Patāka Swami, His Holiness Bhakti Caitanya Swami, His Grace Brihat Mṛdaṅga Prabhu, His Grace Swarūpa Dāmodara Prabhu, Śrīmān Nithiananda Moodley, and Śrīmatī Roshnee Chandanram who all helped in various ways to make this publication a success.

I would also like to especially thank Śrīmān Ranjith Ramnarain for his generous contribution towards the printing of this handbook. May Lord

Kṛṣṇa bestow upon him further advancement in Kṛṣṇa consciousness. Hare Kṛṣṇa.

Rāmānujāchārya Dās

Śrī Gaura Pūrṇimā

2 March, 1999
ISKCON Durban
South Africa

Vaiṣṇava Songs and Prayers

Śrīla Prabhupāda Praṇati

nama oṁ viṣṇu-pādāya
kṛṣṇa-preṣṭhāya bhū-tale
śrīmate bhaktivedānta-
svāmin iti nāmine

namaḥ—obeisances; *oṁ*—address; *viṣṇu-pādāya*—unto him who is at the feet of Viṣṇu; *kṛṣṇa-preṣṭhāya*—unto him who is very dear to Lord Kṛṣṇa; *bhū-tale*—on the earth; *śrīmate*—all-beautiful; *bhakti-vedānta svāmin*—A.C. Bhaktivedanta Swami; *iti*—thus; *nāmine*—who is named.

I offer my respectful obeisances unto His Divine Grace A.C. Bhaktivedanta Swami Prabhupāda, who is very dear to Lord Kṛṣṇa, having taken shelter at His lotus feet.

namas te sārasvate deve
gaura-vāṇī-pracāriṇe
nirviśeṣa-śūnyavādī-
pāścātya-deśa-tāriṇe

namaḥ—obeisances; *te*—unto you; *sārasvate deve*—servant of Bhaktisiddhānta Sarasvatī Gosvāmī; *gaura-vāṇī*—the message of Lord Caitanya; *pracāriṇe*—who are preaching;

nirviśeṣa—(from) impersonalism; *śūnya-vādī*—(from) voidism; *pāścātya*—Western; *deśa*—countries; *tāriṇe*—who are delivering.

Our respectful obeisances are unto you, O spiritual master, servant of Sarasvatī Gosvāmī. You are kindly preaching the message of Lord Caitanyadeva and delivering the Western countries, which are filled with impersonalism and voidism.

Śrī Vaiṣṇava Praṇāma

vāñchā-kalpatarubhyaś ca
kṛpā-sindhubhya eva ca
patitānāṁ pāvanebhyo
vaiṣṇavebhyo namo namaḥ

vāñchā-kalpa-tarubhyaḥ—who are desire trees; *ca*—and; *kṛpā*—(of) mercy; *sindhubhyaḥ*—who are oceans; *eva*—certainly; *ca*—and; *patitānām*—of the fallen souls; *pāvanebhyaḥ*—who are the purifiers; *vaiṣṇavebhaḥ*—unto the Vaiṣṇavas; *namaḥ namaḥ*—repeated obeisances.

I offer my respectful obeisances unto all the Vaiṣṇava devotees of the Lord. They are just like desire trees who can fulfill the desires of everyone, and they are full of compassion for the fallen conditioned souls.

Śrī Gaurāṅga Praṇāma

namo mahā-vadānyāya
kṛṣṇa-prema pradāya te
kṛṣṇāya kṛṣṇa-caitanya-
nāmne gaura-tviṣe namaḥ

namaḥ—obeisances; *mahā-vadānyāya*—who is most munificent and charitably disposed; *kṛṣṇa-prema*—love of Kṛṣṇa; *pradāya*—who can give; *te*—unto You; *kṛṣṇāya*—the original Personality of Godhead; *kṛṣṇa-caitanya-nāmne*—under the name Kṛṣṇa Caitanya; *gaura-tviṣe*—whose complexion is the golden complexion of Śrīmatī Rādhārāṇī; *namaḥ*—obeisances.

O most munificent incarnation! You are Kṛṣṇa Himself appearing as Śrī Kṛṣṇa Caitanya Mahāprabhu. You have assumed the golden color of Śrīmatī Rādhārāṇī, and You are widely distributing pure love of Kṛṣṇa. We offer our respectful obeisances unto You.

—*Śrī Caitanya-caritāmṛta, Madhya* 19.53

(Śrīla Rūpa Gosvāmī recited the above verse when he met Śrī Caitanya Mahāprabhu at Prayāga.)

Śrī Govinda Praṇāma

namo brahmaṇya-devāya
go-brāhmaṇa-hitāya ca
jagad-dhitāya kṛṣṇāya
govindāya namo namaḥ

namaḥ—all obeisances; *brahmaṇya-devāya*—to the Lord worshipable by persons in brahminical culture; *go-brāhmaṇa*—for cows and *brāhmaṇas*; *hitāya*—beneficial; *ca*—also; *jagat-hitāya*—to one who always is benefitting the whole world; *kṛṣṇāya*—unto Kṛṣṇa; *govindāya*—unto Govinda; *namaḥ namaḥ*—repeated obeisances.

Let me offer my respectful obeisances unto Lord Kṛṣṇa, who is the worshipable Deity for all brahminical men, who is the well-wisher of cows and brāhmaṇas, and who is always benefitting the whole world. I offer my repeated obeisances to the Personality of Godhead, known as Kṛṣṇa and Govinda.

—*Viṣṇu Purāṇa* 1.19.65

(Śrī Caitanya Mahāprabhu recited the above verse while He was dancing before Lord Jagannātha during the Ratha-yātrā in Puri. See *Śrī Caitanya-caritāmṛta, Madhya* 13.77.)

Śrī Bhāgavata Praṇāma

kṛṣṇe sva-dhāmopagate
dharma-jñānādibhiḥ saha
kalau naṣṭa-dṛśām eṣa
purāṇārko 'dhunoditaḥ

kṛṣṇe—in Kṛṣṇa's; *sva-dhāma*—own abode; *upagate*—having returned; *dharma*—religion; *jñāna*—knowledge; *ādibhiḥ*—combined together; *saha*—along with; *kalau*—in the Kali-yuga; *naṣṭa-dṛśām*—of persons who have lost their sight; *eṣaḥ*—all these; *purāṇa-arkaḥ*—the *Purāṇa* which is brilliant like the sun; *adhunā*—just now; *uditaḥ*—has arisen.

This Bhāgavata Purāṇa is as brilliant as the sun, and it has arisen just after the departure of Lord Kṛṣṇa to His own abode, accompanied by religion, knowledge, etc. Persons who have lost their vision due to the dense darkness of ignorance in the age of Kali shall get light from this Purāṇa.

—*Śrīmad-Bhāgavatan* 1.3.43

Pañca-tattva Mahā-mantra

(jaya) śrī-kṛṣṇa-caitanya
prabhu nityānanda
śrī-advaita gadādhara
śrīvāsādi-gaura-bhakta-vṛnda

jaya—victory, all glories; *śrī-kṛṣṇa-caitanya*—Śrī Caitanya Mahāprabhu (Kṛṣṇa Himself); *prabhu nityānanda*—Lord Nityānanda (Balarāma Himself); *śrī-advaita*—Śrī Advaita Prabhu (an incarnation of Mahā-Viṣṇu); *gadādhara*—Śrī Gadādhara (an expansion of Rādhārāṇī); *śrīvāsa*—Śrīvāsa Prabhu (an expansion of Nārada Muni); *ādi*—headed by; *gaura*—of Lord Caitanya; *bhakta-vṛnda*—devotees.

All glories to Śrī Caitanya Mahāprabhu accompanied by His eternal associates Śrī Nityānanda Prabhu, Śrī Advaita Prabhu, Śrī Gadādhara Prabhu and all of His devotees headed by Śrīvāsa Prabhu.

(We first offer our obeisances to Śrī Caitanya Mahāprabhu by chanting this Pañca-tattva *mantra*; then we chant the Hare Kṛṣṇa *mahā-mantra*. There are ten offenses in the chanting of the Hare Kṛṣṇa *mahā-mantra*, but these are not considered in the chanting of the Pañca-tattva *mantra.* Śrī Caitanya Mahāprabhu is known as *mahā-vadānyāvatara,* the most magnanimous incarnation, for He does not consider the offenses of the fallen souls. Thus we derive the full benefit of chanting the Hare Kṛṣṇa *mahā-mantra* by first chanting the Pañca-tattva *mantra.*)

Hare Kṛṣṇa Mahā-mantra

hare kṛṣṇa hare kṛṣṇa
kṛṣṇa kṛṣṇa hare hare
hare rāma hare rāma
rāma rāma hare hare

hare—O Harā, the internal, pleasure potency of the Lord (Rādhārāṇī, Sītā, etc.); *kṛṣṇa*—O Kṛṣṇa! O all-attractive person!; *rāma*—O Rāma! O You who enjoy supreme transcendental pleasure! (may refer to Lord Rāmacandra, Lord Balarāma or Lord Kṛṣṇa).

My dear Lord Kṛṣṇa, my dear Lord Rāma, O energy of the Lord, Harā, kindly engage me in Your service.

Śrī Śrī Gurv-aṣṭaka

by Śrīla Viśvanātha Cakravartī Ṭhākura

Śrīla Viśvanātha Cakravartī Ṭhākura, who appeared in the middle of the seventeenth century, is a great spiritual master in the Kṛṣṇa conscious chain of *gurus* and disciples. He says, "One who, with great care and attention, loudly recites these beautiful prayers to the spiritual master during the *brāhma-muhūrta* (the one and one-half hour period just before sunrise) obtains direct service to Kṛṣṇa, the Lord of Vṛndāvana, at the time of death."

(1)

saṁsāra-dāvānala-līḍha-loka-
trāṇāya kāruṇya-ghanāghanatvam
prāptasya kalyāṇa-guṇārṇavasya
vande guroḥ śrī-caraṇāravindam

(2)

mahāprabhoḥ kīrtana-nṛtya-gīta-
vāditra-mādyan-manaso rasena
romāñca-kampāśru-taraṅga-bhājo
vande guroḥ śrī-caraṇāravindam

(3)

śrī-vigrahārādhana-nitya-nānā-
śṛṅgāra-tān-mandira-mārjanādau
yuktasya bhaktāṁś ca niyuñjato 'pi
vande guroḥ śrī-caraṇāravindam

(4)

catur-vidha-śrī-bhagavat-prasāda-
svādv-anna-tṛptān hari-bhakta-saṅghān
kṛtvaiva tṛptiṁ bhajataḥ sadaiva
vande guroḥ śrī-caraṇāravindam

(5)

śrī-rādhikā-mādhavayor apāra-
mādhurya-līlā-guṇa-rūpa-nāmnām
prati-kṣaṇāsvādana-lolupasya
vande guroḥ śrī-caraṇāravindam

(6)

nikuñja-yūno rati-keli-siddhyai
yā yālibhir yuktir apekṣaṇīyā
tatrāti-dākṣyād ati-vallabhasya
vande guroḥ śrī-caraṇāravindam

(7)

sākṣād-dharitvena samasta-śāstrair
uktas tathā bhāvyata eva sadbhiḥ
kintu prabhor yaḥ priya eva tasya
vande guroḥ śrī-caraṇāravindam

(8)

yasya prasādād bhagavat-prasādo
yasyāprasādān na gatiḥ kuto 'pi
dhyāyan stuvaṁs tasya yaśas tri-sandhyaṁ
vande guroḥ śrī-caraṇāravindam

(1) *saṁsāra*—(of) material existence; *dāva-anala*—(by) the forest fire; *līḍha*—afflicted; *loka*—people; *trāṇāya*—to deliver; *kāruṇya*—of mercy; *ghanāghana-tvam*—the quality of a cloud; *prāptasya*—who has obtained; *kalyāṇa*—auspicious; *guṇa*—(of) qualities; *arṇavasya*—who is an ocean; *vande*—I offer obeisances; *guroḥ*—of my spiritual master; *śrī*—auspicious; *caraṇa-aravindam*—unto the lotus feet.

The spiritual master is receiving benediction from the ocean of mercy. Just as a cloud pours water on a forest fire to extinguish it, so the spiritual master delivers the materially afflicted world by extinguishing the blazing fire of material existence. I offer my respectful obeisances unto the lotus feet of such a spiritual master, who is an ocean of auspicious qualities.

(2) *mahāprabhoḥ*—of Lord Caitanya Mahāprabhu; *kīrtana*—(by) chanting; *nṛtya*—dancing; *gīta*—singing; *vāditra*—playing musical instruments; *mādyat*—gladdened; *manasaḥ*—whose mind; *rasena*—due to the mellows of pure devotion; *roma-añca*—standing of the hair; *kampa*—quivering of the body; *aśru-taraṅga*—torrents of tears; *bhājaḥ*—who feels.

Chanting the holy name, dancing in ecstasy, singing and playing musical instruments, the spiritual master is always gladdened by the *saṅkīrtana* movement of Lord Caitanya Mahāprabhu. Because he is relishing the mellows of pure devotion within his mind, sometimes his hair stands on end, He feels quivering in his body, and tears flow from his eyes like waves. I offer my respectful obeisances unto the lotus feet of such a spiritual master.

(3) *śrī-vigraha*—(of) the *arca-vigraha* (Deities); *ārādhana*—the worship; *nitya*—daily; *nānā*—(with) various; *śṛṅgāra*—clothing and ornaments; *tat*—of the Lord; *mandira*—(of) the temple; *mārjana-ādau*—in the cleaning, etc.; *yuktasya*—who is engaged; *bhaktān*—his disciples; *ca*—and; *niyuñjataḥ*—who engages; *api*—also.

The spiritual master is always engaged in the temple worship of Śrī Śrī Rādhā and Kṛṣṇa. He also engages his disciples in such worship. They dress the Deities in beautiful clothes and ornaments, clean Their temple, and perform other similar worship of the Lord. I offer my respectful obeisances unto the lotus feet of such a spiritual master.

(4) *catuḥ*—four; *vidha*—kinds; *śrī*—holy; *bhagavat-prasāda*—which have been offered to Krsna; *svādu*—palatable; *anna*—(by) foods; *tṛptān*—spiritually satisfied; *hari*—(of) Kṛṣṇa; *bhakta-saṅghān*—the devotees; *kṛtvā*—having made; *eva*—thus; *tṛptim*—satisfaction; *bhajataḥ*—who feels; *sadā*—always; *eva*—certainly.

The spiritual master is always offering Kṛṣṇa four kinds of delicious food [analyzed as that which is licked, chewed, drunk and sucked]. When the spiritual master sees that the devotees are satisfied by eating *bhagavat-prasāda*, he is satisfied. I offer my respectful obeisances unto the lotus feet of such a spiritual master.

(5) *śrī-rādhikā*—(of) Śrīmatī Rādhārāṇī; *mādhavayoḥ*—of Lord Mādhava (Kṛṣṇa); *apāra*—unlimited; *mādhurya*—conjugal; *līlā*—pastimes; *guṇa*—qualities; *rūpa*—forms; *nāmnām*—of the holy names; *prati-kṣaṇa*—at every moment; *āsvādana*—relishing; *lolupasya*—who aspires after.

The spiritual master is always eager to hear and chant about the unlimited conjugal pastimes of Rādhikā and Mādhava, and Their qualities, names and forms. The spiritual master aspires to relish these at every moment. I offer my respectful obeisances unto the lotus feet of such a spiritual master.

(6) *nikuñja-yūnaḥ*—of Rādhā and Kṛṣṇa; *rati*—(of) conjugal love; *keli*—(of) pastimes; *siddhyai*—for the perfection; *yā yā*—whatever; *ālibhiḥ*—by the *gopīs; yuktiḥ*—arrangements; *apekṣaṇīyā*—desirable; *tatra*—in that connection; *ati-dākṣyāt*—because of being very expert; *ati-vallabhasya*—who is very dear.

The spiritual master is very dear, because he is expert in assisting the *gopīs*, who at different times make different tasteful arrangements for the perfection of Rādhā and Kṛṣṇa's conjugal loving affairs within the groves of Vṛndāvana. I offer my respectful obeisances unto the lotus feet of such a spiritual master.

(7) *sākṣāt*—directly; *hari-tvena*—with the quality of Hari; *samasta*—all; *śāstraiḥ*—by scriptures; *uktaḥ*—acknowledged; *tathā*—thus; *bhāvyate*—is considered; *eva*—also; *sadbhiḥ*—by great saintly persons; *kintu*—however; *prabhoḥ*—to the Lord; *yaḥ*—who; *priyaḥ*—dear; *eva*—certainly; *tasya*—of him (the *guru*).

The spiritual master is to be honored as much as the Supreme Lord, because he is the most confidential servitor of the Lord. This is acknowledged in all revealed scriptures and followed by all authorities. Therefore I offer my respectful obeisances unto the lotus feet of such a spiritual master, who is a bonafide representative of Śrī Hari [Kṛṣṇa].

(8) *yasya*—of whom (the spiritual master); *prasādāt*—by the grace; *bhagavat*—(of) Kṛṣṇa; *prasādaḥ*—the mercy; *yasya*—of whom; *aprasādāt*—without the grace; *na*—not; *gatiḥ*—means of advancement; *kutaḥ api*—from anywhere; *dhyāyan*—meditating upon; *stuvan*—praising; *tasya*—of him (the spiritual master); *yaśaḥ*—the glory; *tri-sandhyam*—three times a day (sunrise, noon and sunset).

By the mercy of the spiritual master one receives the benediction of Kṛṣṇa. Without the grace of the spiritual master, one cannot make any advancement. Therefore, I should always remember and praise the spiritual master. At least three times a day I should offer my respectful obeisances unto the lotus feet of my spiritual master.

Śrī Nṛsiṁha Praṇāma and Prayer to Lord Nṛsiṁha

(1)

namas te narasiṁhāya
prahlādāhlāda-dāyine
hiraṇykaśipor vakṣaḥ-
śila-ṭaṅka-nakhālaye

(2)

ito nṛsiṁhaḥ parato nṛsiṁho
yato yato yāmi tato nṛsiṁhaḥ
bahir nṛsiṁho hṛdaye nṛsiṁho
nṛsiṁham ādiṁ śaraṇaṁ prapadye

(3)

tava kara-kamala-vare nakham adbhuta śṛṅgaṁ
dalita-hiraṇyakaśipu-tanu-bhṛṅgam
keśava dhṛta-narahari-rūpa jaya jagadīsa hare

(4)

bhakti-vighna-vināśaka
nṛsiṁhadeva bhagavān kī jay.
bhakta śreṣṭha prahlāda mahārāja kī jay.

(1) *namaḥ*—obeisances; *te*—unto You; *nara-siṁhāya*—unto Lord Narasiṁha; *prahlāda*—(to) Prahlāda Mahārāja; *āhlāda*—(of) joy; *dāyine*—the giver; *hiraṇyakaśipoḥ*—of Hiraṇyakaśipu; *vakṣaḥ*—chest; *śila*—(on) the stonelike; *ṭaṅka*—chisels; *nakha-ālaye*—whose nails.

I offer my obeisances to Lord Nṛsiṁha, who gives joy to Prahlāda Mahārāja and whose nails are like chisels on the stonelike chest of the demon Hiraṇyakaśipu.

(2) *itaḥ*—here; *nṛsiṁhaḥ*—Lord Nṛsiṁha; *parataḥ*—there; *nṛsiṁhaḥ*— Lord Nṛsiṁha; *yataḥ yataḥ*—wherever; *yāmi*—I go; *tataḥ*—there; *nṛsiṁhaḥ*—Lord Nṛsiṁha; *bahiḥ*—externally; *nṛsiṁhaḥ*—Lord Nṛsiṁha; *hṛdaye*—in the heart; *nṛsiṁhaḥ*—Lord Nṛsiṁha; *nṛsiṁham*—to Lord Nṛsiṁha; *ādim*—the origin; *śaraṇam*—the supreme refuge; *prapadye*—I surrender.

Lord Nṛsiṁha is here and also there. Wherever I go Lord Nṛsiṁha is there. He is in the heart and is outside as well. I surrender to Lord Nṛsiṁha, the origin of all things and the supreme refuge.

(3) *tava*—Your; *kara-kamala-vare*—on the beautiful lotus hands; *nakham*—the nails; *adbhuta*—wonderful; *śṛṅgam*—pointed; *dalita*—ripped apart; *hiraṇyakaśipu*—(of) Hiraṇyakaśipu; *tanu*—body; *bhṛṅgam*—wasplike; *keśava*—O Lord Keśava who posseses fine hair! *dhṛta*—who have assumed; *nara*—man; *hari*—lion; *rūpa*—form; *jaya*—all glories to You; *jagat-īśa*—O Lord of the universe! *hare*—O Lord Hari!

O Keśava! O Lord of the universe! O Lord Hari, who have assumed the form of half-man, half-lion! All glories to You! Just as one can easily crush a wasp between one's fingernails, so in the same way the body of the wasplike demon Hiraṇyakaśipu has been ripped apart by the wonderful pointed nails on Your beautiful lotus hands.

(4) *bhakti*—(on the path of) devotional service; *vighna*—obstacles; *vināśaka*—the detroyer; *nṛsiṁhadeva*—Nṛsiṁhadeva; *bhagavān*—Lord; *kī jaya*—all glories to; *bhakta*—the devotee; *śreṣṭha*—topmost; *prahlāda mahārāja*—Prahlāda Mahārāja; *kī jaya*—all glories to.

All glories to Lord Nṛsiṁadeva who is the destroyer of obstacles on the path of devotional service. All glories to the topmost devotee, Prahlāda Mahārāja.

(The first two verses, from the *Nṛsiṁha Purāṇa*, were recited by Śrī Caitanya Mahāprabhu while offering obeisances to the Deity of Lord Nṛsiṁhadeva in the Jagannātha temple at Puri. [*Śrī Caitanya-caritāmṛta, Antya* 16.52-53] The third verse is from the *Śrī Daśāvatāra-stotra* which is in the *Gīta-govinda* by Jayadeva Gosvāmī.)

Śrī Tulasī Praṇāma

vṛndāyai tulasī-devyai
priyāyai keśavasya ca
viṣṇu-bhakti-prade devi
satyavatyai namo namaḥ

vṛndāyai—unto Vṛndā; *tulasī-devyai*—unto Tulasī Devī; *priyāyai*—who is dear; *keśavasya*—to Lord Keśava; *ca*—and; *viṣṇu-bhakti*—devotional service to Lord Viṣṇu; *prade*—who bestows; *devi*—O goddess; *satyavatyai*—unto Satyavatī (the truthful); *namaḥ namaḥ*—repeated obeisances.

I offer my repeated obeisances unto Vṛndā, Śrīmatī Tulasī Devī, who is very dear to Lord Keśava. O goddess, you bestow devotional service to Lord Viṣṇu and possess the highest truth.

Śrī Tulasī-kīrtana

(1)

namo namaḥ tulasī! kṛṣṇa-preyasī
(braje) rādhā-kṛṣṇa-sevā pābo ei abhilāṣī

(2)

je tomāra śaraṇa loy, tāra vāñchā pūrṇa hoy
kṛpā kori' koro tāre bṛndābana-bāsī

(3)

mor ei abhilāṣ, bilās kuñje dio bās
nayane heribo sadā jugala-rūpa-rāśī

(4)

ei nivedana dharo, sakhīr anugata koro
sebā-adhikāra diye koro nija dāsī

(5)

dīna kṛṣṇa-dāse koy, ei jena mora hoy
śrī-rādhā-govinda-preme sadā jena bhāsi

WORD MEANINGS AND TRANSLATIONS

(1) *namo namaḥ*—bowing again and again; *tulasī*—O Tulasī!; *kṛṣṇa-preyasī*—O beloved of Kṛṣṇa! *braje*—in Vraja; *rādhā-kṛṣṇa-sevā*—the service of Śrī Śrī Rādhā and Kṛṣṇa; *pābo*—I shall get; *ei*—this; *abhilāṣī*—aspirant devotee.

O Tulasī, beloved of Kṛṣṇa, I bow before you again and again. My desire is to obtain the service of Śrī Śrī Rādhā and Kṛṣṇa (in Vraja).

(2) *je*—whoever; *tomāra*—your; *śaraṇa*—shelter; *loy*—takes; *tāra*—his; *vāñchā*—desires; *pūrṇa hoy*—are fulfilled; *kṛpā kori'*—being merciful; *koro*—you make; *tāre*—him; *bṛndābana-bāsī*—a resident of Vṛndāvana.

Whoever takes shelter of you has his wishes fulfilled. Bestowing your mercy upon him, you make him a resident of Vṛndāvana.

(3) *mora*—my; *ei*—this; *abhilāṣ*—desire; *bilās kuñje*—in the pleasure groves; *dio*—please give; *bās*—a residence; *nayane*—with my eyes; *heribo*—I will behold; *sadā*—always; *jugala-rūpa-rāśi*—the beautiful pastimes of Rādhā and Kṛṣṇa.

My desire is that you will also grant me a residence in the pleasure groves of Śrī Vṛndāvana-dhāma. Thus, within my vision I will always behold the beautiful pastimes of Rādhā and Kṛṣṇa.

(4) *ei*—this; *nivedana*—request; *dharo*—please accept; *sakhīr* —of the cowherd damsels of Vraja; *anugata koro*—make me a follower; *sevā*—of

service; *adhikāra*—privilege; *diye*—giving; *koro*—please make; *nija*—your own; *dāsī*—maidservant.

I beg you to make me a follower of the cowherd damsels of Vraja. Please give me the privilege of devotional service and make me your own maid-servant.

(5) *dīna*—fallen and lowly; *kṛṣṇa-dāse*—by (this) servant of Kṛṣṇa; *koy*—prayed; *ei*—this; *jena*—just like; *mora hoy*—is mine; *śrī-rādhā-govinda-preme*—in the love of Śri Rādhā and Govinda; *sadā*—always; *jena*—just like; *bhāsi*—swimming.

This very fallen and lowly servant of Kṛṣṇa prays, "May I always swim in the love of Śrī Rādhā and Govinda."

Śrī Tulasī Pradakṣiṇa Mantra

yāni kāni ca pāpāni
brahma-hatyādikāni ca
tāni tāni praṇaśyanti
pradakṣiṇaḥ pade pade

yāni kāni—whatever; *ca*—and; *pāpāni*—sins; *brahma-hatya*—killing of a *brāhmaṇa*; *ādikāni*—and so on; *ca*—also; *tāni tāni*—all of them; *praṇa-*

śyanti—are destroyed; *pradakṣiṇaḥ*—(by) circumambulation (of Tulasī Devī); *pade pade*—at every step.

By circumambulation of Śrīmatī Tulasī Devī all the sins that one may have committed are destroyed at every step, even the sin of killing a *brāhmaṇa*.

Śrī Brahma-saṁhitā

(1)

veṇuṁ kvaṇantam aravinda-dalāyatākṣaṁ
barhāvataṁsam asitāmbuda-sundarāṅgam
kandarpa-koṭi-kamanīya-viśeṣa-śobhaṁ
govindam ādi-puruṣaṁ tam ahaṁ bhajāmi

(2)

aṅgāni yasya sakalendriya-vṛtti-manti
paśyanti pānti kalayanti ciraṁ jaganti
ānanda-cinmaya-sad-ujjvala-vigrahasya
govindam ādi-puruṣaṁ tam ahaṁ bhajāmi

WORD MEANINGS AND TRANSLATIONS

(1) *veṇuṁ*—the flute; *kvaṇantam*—playing; *aravinda-dala*—(like) lotus petals; *āyata*—blooming; *akṣam*—whose eyes; *barha*—a peacock's feather; *avataṁsam*—whose ornament on the head; *asita-ambuda*—(tinged with the hue of) blue clouds;

sundara—beautiful; *aṅgam*—whose figure; *kandarpa*—of Cupids; *koṭi*—millions; *kamanīya*—charming; *viśeṣa*—unique; *śobham*—whose loveliness; *govindam*—Govinda; *ādi-puruṣam*—the original person; *tam*—Him; *aham*—I; *bhajāmi*—worship.

I worship Govinda, the primeval Lord, who is adept in playing on His flute, with blooming eyes like lotus petals with head decked with a peacock's feather, with the figure of beauty tinged with the hue of blue clouds, and His unique loveliness charming millions of Cupids.

(2) *aṅgāni*—the limbs; *yasya*—of whom; *sakala-indriya*—of all the organs; *vṛtti-manti*—possessing the functions; *paśyanti*—see; *pānti*—maintain; *kalayanti*—manifest; *ciram*—eternally; *jaganti*—the universes; *ānanda*—bliss; *cit*—truth; *maya*—full of; *sat*—substantiality; *ujjvala*—full of dazzling splendor; *vigrahasya*—whose form.

I worship Govinda, the primeval Lord, whose transcendental form is full of bliss, truth and substantiality, and is thus full of the most dazzling splendor. Each of the limbs of that transcendental form possesses in Himself, the full-fledged functions of all the organs, and eternally sees, maintains and manifests the infinite universes, both spiritual and mundane.

(The above two verses are verses 30 and 32 from the *Brahma-saṁhitā*. They are sung by the devotees at the time of greeting the Deities in the temple at 7 a.m.)

Śrī Guru-vandanā

The Worship of Śrī Guru
by Śrīla Narottama dāsa Ṭhākura

(1)

śrī-guru-caraṇa-padma, kevala-bhakati-sadma,
bando mui sāvadhāna mate
jāhāra prasāde bhāi, e bhava toriyā jāi,
kṛṣṇa-prāpti hoy jāhā ha'te

(2)

guru-mukha-padma-vākya, cittete koriyā aikya,
ār nā koriho mane āśā
śrī-guru-caraṇe rati, ei se uttama-gati
je prasāde pūre sarva āśā

(3)

cakhu-dān dilo jei, janme janme prabhu sei,
divya-jñān hṛde prokāśito
prema-bhakti jāhā hoite, avidyā vināśa jāte,
vede gāy jāhāra carito

(4)

śrī-guru karuṇā-sindhu, adhama janāra bandhu,
lokanāth lokera jīvana
(śrīla prabhupād lokera jīvana)
hā hā prabhu koro doyā, deho more pada-chāyā,
ebe jaś ghuṣuk tribhuvana

(dui pade loilo śaraṇa)
(śrīla prabhupāda patita-pāvana)

WORD MEANINGS AND TRANSLATIONS

(1) *śrī-guru*—the spiritual master; *caraṇa*—feet; *padma*—lotus; *kevala*—only (pure); *bhakati*—(of) devotional service; *sadma*—abode; *bando*—bow down; *mui*—I; *sāvadhāna mate*—with great care and attention; *jāhāra*—whose; *prasāde*—grace, mercy; *bhāi*—O my dear brothers! *e*—this; *bhava*—material existence; *toriyā jāi*—crossing over; *kṛṣṇa prāpti*—obtaining Kṛṣṇa; *hoy*—becomes; *jāhā ha'te*—by which.

The lotus feet of our spiritual master are the only way by which we can attain pure devotional service. I bow down to his lotus feet with great awe and reverence. By his grace one can cross the ocean of material suffering and obtain the mercy of Kṛṣna.

(2) *guru*—the spiritual master; *mukha*—mouth; *padma*—lotus; *vākya*—the words; *cittete*—in the heart; *koriyā*—making; *aikya*—oneness; *ār*—any other; *nā*—not; *koriho*—have; *mane*—in the mind; *āśā*—desire; *śrī-guru*—of the spiritual master; *caraṇe*—to the lotus feet; *rati*—attachment; *ei*—this; *se*—that; *uttama*—best; *gati*—course of action; *je prasāde*—by whose mercy; *pūre*—(become) fulfilled; *sarva*—all; *āśā*—hopes, desires.

My only wish is to have my consciousness purified by the words emanating from his lotus mouth. Attachment to his lotus feet is the perfection that fulfills all desires.

(3) *cakhu*—(of) transcendental; *dān*—the gift; *dilo*—gave; *jei*—who; *janme janme*—birth after birth; *prabhu*—(my) lord; *sei*—he (is); *divya*—divine; *jñān*—knowledge; *hṛde*—within the heart; *prokāśito*—(is) revealed; *prema-bhakti*—loving devotional service; *jāhā hoite*—from whom; *avidyā*—ignorance; *vināśa*—destroyed; *jāte*—by whom; *vede*—in the Vedas; *gāy*—is sung; *jāhāra*—whose; *carito*—character.

He opens my darkened eyes and fills my heart with transcendental knowledge. He is my lord birth after birth. From him ecstatic *prema* emanates. By him ignorance is destroyed. The Vedic scriptures sing of his character.

(4) *śrī-guru*—O spiritual master! *karuṇā-sindhu*—O ocean of mercy! *adhama-janāra*—of the fallen souls; *bandhu*—the friend; *lokanātha*—O Lokanātha (the spiritual master of Śrīla Narottama dāsa Ṭhākura) or the spiritual master of the people; *lokera*—of the people; *jīvana*—the life; *hā hā prabhu*—O master! *koro doyā*—please be merciful; *deho*—please give; *more*—to me; *pada-chāyā*—the shade of (your lotus) feet; *ebe*—now; *jaś*—fame; *ghuṣuk*—may it be proclaimed; *tri-bhuvana*—(throughout) the three worlds;

Our spiritual master is the ocean of mercy, the friend of the poor, and the lord and master of the devotees. O master, please be merciful unto us. Give us the shade of your lotus feet. Your fame is spread all over the three worlds. We take shelter at your lotus feet.

(extra words) *dui pade*—at his two feet; *loilo śaraṇa* —we have taken shelter; *śrīla prabhu-pāda*—Śrīla Prabhupāda; *patita*—of the fallen; *pāvana*—the savior.

Jaya Rādhā-Mādhava

by Śrīla Bhaktivinoda Ṭhākura

(jaya) rādhā-mādhava (jaya) kuñja-bihārī
(jaya) gopī-jana-vallabha (jaya) giri-bara-dhārī
jaśodā-nandana, braja-jana-rañjana,
jāmuna-tīra-vana-cārī

jaya—all glories to; *rādhā*—Rādhārāṇī; *mādhava*—Mādhava (Kṛṣṇa, the husband of the goddess of fortune [*mā*—the goddess of fortune; *dhava*—the husband]); *kuñja*—(in) the groves (of Vṛndāvana); *bihārī*—the enjoyer of pastimes; *gopī-jana*—(of) the cowherd maidens; *vallabha*—the lover and beloved; *giri*—(of) the hill (Govardhana); *bara*—great; *dhārī*—the holder; *jaśodā*—Mother Yaśodā; *nandana*—the beloved son; *braja-jana*—(of) the inhabitants of Braja; *rañjana*—the delighter; *jāmuna*—(of) the River Yamunā; *tīra*—(along) the banks; *vana*—(in) the forests; *cārī*—the wanderer.

Kṛṣṇa is the lover of Rādhā. He displays many amorous pastimes in the groves of Vṛndāvana. He is the lover and beloved of the cowherd maidens of Vraja, the holder of the great hill named Govardhana, the beloved son of Mother Yaśodā, the delighter of the inhabitants of Vraja, and He wanders in the forests along the banks of the River Yamunā.

(Śrīla Prabhupāda was very fond of this song, and sang it just before his lectures. In Allahabad and Gorakhpur Śrīla Prabhupāda fell into a trance after singing the first two lines, and after some time he came back into external consciousness and said, "Now just chant Hare Kṛṣṇa." Śrīla Prabhupāda said that this song is "a picture of Vṛndāvana. Everything is there—Śrīmatī Rādhārāṇī, Vṛndāvana, Govardhana, Yaśodā, and all the cowherd boys.")

Invocation

(Recited at the beginning of class)

oṁ namo bhagavate vāsudevāya

oṁ—O my Lord; *namaḥ*—I offer my respectful obeisances; *bhagavate*—unto the Supreme Personality of Godhead; *vāsudevāya*—unto Vāsudeva, Kṛṣṇa, the son of Vasudeva.

O my Lord, Śrī Kṛṣṇa, the son of Vasudeva, I offer my respectful obeisances unto You.

(This *mantra* is the invocation at the beginnings of the First and Second Cantos of *Śrīmad-Bhāga-*

vatam. Dhruva Mahārāja was initiated into the chanting of this *mantra* by Nārada Muni. See *Śrīmad-Bhāgavatam* 4.8.53-54.)

Gaura-ārati

by Śrīla Bhaktivinoda Ṭhākura

(1)

jaya jaya gorācānder āratiko śobhā
jāhnavī-taṭa-vane jaga-mana-lobhā
(gaurāṅger āratiko śobhā,
jaga-jana-mana-lobhā)

(2)

dakhiṇe nitāicānd, bāme gadādhara
nikaṭe adwaita, śrīnivāsa chatra-dhara

(3)

bosiyāche gorācānd ratna-siṁhāsane
ārati korena brahmā-ādi deva-gaṇe

(4)

narahari-ādi kori' cāmara ḍhulāya
sañjaya-mukunda-bāsu-ghoṣa-ādi gāya

(5)

śaṅkha bāje ghaṇṭā bāje bāje karatāla
madhura mṛdaṅga bāje parama rasāla

(śaṅkha bāje ghaṇṭā bāje,
madhur madhur madhur bāje)

(6)

bahu-koṭi candra jini' vadana ujjwala
gala-deśe bana-mālā kore jhalamala

(7)

śiva-śuka-nārada preme gada-gada
bhakativinoda dekhe gorāra sampada

WORD MEANINGS AND TRANSLATIONS

(1) *jaya jaya*—all glories, all glories; *gorācānder*—of the moonlike Lord Caitanya; *āratiko*—the *ārati* ceremony; *śobha*—beautiful; *jāhnāvī*—(of) the Ganges; *taṭa*—(on) the bank; *vane*—in a grove; *jaga*—(of) all the living entities in the universe; *mana*—the minds; *lobhā*—attracting; *jaga-jana*—the people of the universe.

All glories, all glories to the beautiful *ārati* ceremony of Lord Caitanya. This Gaura-ārati is taking place in a grove on the bank of the Jāhnavī (Ganges) and is attracting the minds of all living entities in the universe.

(2) *dakhiṇe*—on (Lord Caitanya's) right side; *nitāicānd*—the moonlike Lord Nityānanda; *bāme*

—on (His) left; *gadādhara*—Gadādhara; *nikaṭe*—nearby; *adwaita*—Adwaita Ācārya; *śrīnivāsa*—Śrīnvāsa Ṭhākura; *chatra*—umbrella; *dhara*—the holder.

On Lord Caitanya's right side is Lord Nityānanda, and on His left is Gadādhara. Nearby stands Śrī Advaita, and Śrīvāsa Ṭhākura is holding an umbrella over Lord Caitanya's head.

(3) *bosiyāche*—has sat down; *gorācānd*—Lord Gaura-candra; *ratna*—jeweled; *siṁhāsane*—on a throne; *ārati*—the *ārati* ceremony; *korena*—perform; *brahmā-ādi*—headed by Lord Brahmā; *deva-gaṇe*—the demigods.

Lord Caitanya has sat down on a jeweled throne, and the demigods, headed by Lord Brahmā, perform the *ārati* ceremony.

(4) *narahari-ādi*—Narahari Sarakāra and others; *kori'*—doing; *cāmara*—yak-tail fan; *ḍhulāya*—fanning; *sañjaya*—Sañjaya Paṇḍita; *mukunda*—Mukunda Datta; *bāsu-ghoṣa*—Vāsudeva Ghoṣa; *ādi*—headed by; *gāya*—are singing.

Narahari Sarakāra and other associates of Lord Caitanya fan him with *cāmaras*, and devotees headed by Sañjaya Paṇḍita, Mukunda Datta, and Vāsu Ghoṣa sing sweet *kīrtana.*

(5) *śaṅkha*—conchshells; *bāje*—resound; *ghaṇṭā*—bells and/or gongs; *bāje*—resound; *bāje*—resound; *karatāla*—hand-cymbals; *madhura*—sweet; *mṛdaṅga*—*mṛdaṅgas*; *bāje*—resound; *parama*—supremely; *rasāla*—sweet and relishable.

Conchshells, bells, and *karatālas* resound, and the *mṛdaṅgas* play very sweetly. This *kīrtana* music is supremely sweet and relishable to hear.

(6) *bahu*—many; *koṭi*—millions; *candra*—of moons; *jini'*—conquering; *vadana*—(His) face; *ujjwala*—brilliant; *gala-deśe*—around His neck; *bana-mālā*—the garland of forest flowers; *kore jhalamala*—is shining brightly.

The brilliance of Lord Caitanya's face conquers millions upon millions of moons, and the garland of forest flowers around His neck shines brightly.

(7) *śiva*—Lord Śiva; *śuka*—Śukadeva Gosvāmī; *nārada*—Nārada Muni; *preme*—with ecstacy of transcendental love; *gada-gada*—their voices are choked; *bhakativinoda*—Bhaktivinoda Ṭhākura; *dekhe*—envisions; *gorāra*—of Gorā (Lord Caitanya); *sampada*—the glory.

Lord Śiva, Śukadeva Gosvāmī and Nārada Muni are all there, and their voices are choked with the ecstasy of transcendental love. Thus Bhaktivinoda Ṭhākura envisions the glory of Lord Śrī Caitanya.

Prema-dhvani

1. *jay oṁ viṣṇu-pād paramahaṁsa parivrājakācārya aṣṭottara-śata śrī śrīmad a.c. bhaktivedānta svāmī mahārāj prabhupāda kī jay*

2. *ISKCON-saṁsthāpakācārya śrīla prabhupāda kī jay.* **or** *ISKCON-founder-ācārya śrīla prabhupāda kī jay.*

3. *jay oṁ viṣṇu-pād paramahaṁsa parivrājakācārya aṣṭottara-śata śrī śrīmad bhaktisiddhānta sarasvatī gosvāmī mahārāj prabhupāda kī jay.*

[4] *jay oṁ viṣṇu-pād śrīla gaurakiśor dās bābājī mahārāj kī jay.*

[5] *jay oṁ viṣṇu-pād śrīla saccidānanda bhaktivinod ṭhākur kī jay.*

[6] *jay oṁ viṣṇu-pād śrīla vaiṣṇava-sārvabhauma śrīla jagannāth dās bābājī mahārāj kī jay.*

[7] *jay śrī rūp sanātan bhaṭṭa-raghunāth śrī jīv gopāl bhaṭṭa dās raghunāth ṣaḍ-gosvāmī prabhu kī jay.*

8. *nāmācārya śrīla haridās ṭhākur kī jay.*

9. *ISKCON-vartmāna-guru-vṛnda kī jay.*

10. *ananta koṭi vaiṣṇav-vṛnda kī jay.*

11. *prem-se kaho śrī-kṛṣṇa-caitanya, prabhu nityānanda, śrī-advaita, gadādhar, śrīvāsādi gaura-bhakta-vṛnda kī jay.*

12. *śrī śrī rādhā-kṛṣṇa, gop-gopī-nāth, śyām-kuṇḍ, rādhā-kuṇḍ giri-govardhan kī jay.*

(One may glorify the Deities of the temple at this time.)

13. *śrī navadwīp māyāpur dhām kī jay.*

14. *śrī mathurā vṛndāvan dhām kī jay.*

15. *gaṅgā-mayī kī jay.*

16. *yamunā-mayī kī jay.*

17. *bhakti-devī kī jay.*

18. *tulasī-devī kī jay.*

19. *śrī hari-nām saṅkīrtan kī jay.*

[20] *grantha-rāj śrīmad-bhāgavatam kī jay.*

21. *samaveta bhakta-vṛnda kī jay.*

22. *gaura-premānande hari-hari-bol.*

All glories to the assembled devotees. [three times]

All glories to Śrī Śrī Guru and Gaurāṅga.

Please note: The items whose numbers are in brackets (Nos. 4, 5, 6, 7 and 20) may be omitted for a shorter Prema-dhvani.

WORD MEANINGS AND TRANSLATIONS

(Many of the words and phrases in the successive *prema-dhvani* prayers are repeated. Therefore in order to save space they will not be unnecessarily repeated in the following list of word meanings.)

(1) *jay*—all glories to; *oṁ*—(address); *viṣṇu-pād* —who is situated at the lotus feet of Lord Viṣṇu; *paramahaṁsa*—topmost swanlike devotee, situated on the highest position of *sannyāsa*; *pari-vrājakācārya*—who travels everywhere; *aṣṭa-uttara-śata*—108 (*aṣṭa*—eight; *uttara*—above; *śata* —100); *śrī śrīmad*—(title of respect); *a.*—*Abhay* —fearless; *c.*—*Caraṇa-aravinda*—lotus feet (of the Lord); *bhakti-veda-anta*—one who has attained the ultimate knowledge through devotional service; *svāmī*—master; *mahārāj*—one who has control over his senses just as a king (*mahārāj*) has control over his kingdom; *prabhupāda*—one who has taken the position *(pāda)* of the Lord *(prabhu)*; *kī jay*—all glories to.

All glories to the *ācārya* Oṁ Viṣṇu-pāda 108 Tridaṇḍī Gosvāmī A.C. Bhaktivedanta Swami Prabhupāda, who travels everywhere, preaching the glories of Hari, and who is situated on the highest platform of *sannyāsa.*

(2) *saṁsthāpaka*—founder; *ācārya*—expert spiritual master who teaches by example.

All glories to Śrīla Prabhupāda, the Founder-Ācārya of ISKCON.

(3) *bhakti-siddha-anta*—one who has attained the ultimate perfection through devotional service; *sarasvatī*—(title given for scholarship) the goddess of learning.

All glories to the *ācārya* Oṁ Viṣṇu-pāda 108 Tridaṇḍī Gosvāmī Bhaktisiddhānta Sarasvatī Prabhupāda, who travels everywhere, preaching the glories of Hari, and who is situated on the highest platform of *sannyāsa.*

(4) *gaur*—Lord Caitanya; *kiśor*—youth; *dās*—servant of; *bābājī*—a renounced devotee who practices Kṛṣṇa consciousness in solitude.

All glories to Śrīla Gaurakiśora dāsa Bābājī.

(5) *sat-cit-ānanda*—eternal, full of bliss and knowledge; *bhakti-vinoda*—one who has attained happiness through devotional service; *ṭhākur*—a title of respect.

All glories to Śrīla Sac-cid-ānanda Bhaktivinoda Ṭhākura.

(6) *vaiṣṇava*—(of) the Vaiṣṇavas (devotees of Lord Viṣṇu); *sārvabhauma*—chief; *jagat-nāth*—Lord of the universe.

All glories to Vaiṣṇava-Sārvabhauma Śrīla Jagannātha dāsa Bābājī.

(7) *rūp*—form, beauty; *sanātan*—eternal; *bhaṭṭa* — a title used with the names of learned *brāhmaṇas*; *raghu-nāth*—Lord of the dynasty of Raghu (Lord Rāmacandra); *jīv*—living being; *go-pāl*—protector of the cows (Kṛṣṇa); *ṣaṭ*—six; *gosvāmī*—masters of the senses; *prabhu*—masters.

All glories to the six Gosvāmīs, namely, Śrī Rūpa, Sanātana, Raghunātha Bhaṭṭa, Jīva, Gopāla Bhaṭṭa and Raghunātha Dāsa.

(8) *nāma-ācārya*—spiritual master of the holy name; *hari*—He who takes away (the distress of His devotees); *dās*—servant (of).

All glories to the Nāmācārya Śrīla Haridāsa Ṭhākura.

(9) *vartmāna*—present; *vṛnda*—group.

All glories to the present gurus of ISKCON.

(10) *ananta*—unlimited; *koṭi*—millions; *vṛnda*—group.

All glories to the unlimited millions of Vaiṣṇavas.

(11) *prem-se*—with love; *kaho*—call out.

Call out with love the names of Śrī Kṛṣṇa Caitanya, Prabhu Nityānanda, Śrī Advaita, Śri Gadādhara, Śrīvāsa and all the devotees of Lord Caitanya.

(12) *gop*—the cowherd boys; *gopī*—the cowherd girls; *nāth*—the lord and master; *kuṇḍa*—pond; *giri*—hill.

All glories to Rādhā and Kṛṣṇa, the cowherd boys and girls, Śyāma-kuṇḍa, Rāḍhā-kuṇḍa and Govardhana Hill.

(13 & 14) *dhām*—spiritual abode.

(13) All glories to Śrī Navadvīpa Māyāpura-dhāma.

(14) All glories to Śrī Mathurā Vṛndāvana-dhāma.

(15) All glories to Gaṅgā-devī.

(16) All glories to Yamunā-devī.

(17) All glories to Bhakti-devī.

(18) All glories to Tulasī-devī.

(19) All glories to the congregational chanting of the holy name of Hari.

(20) *grantha*—(of) books; *rāj*—king.

All glories to the king of books, *Śrīmad-Bhāgavatam.*

(21) *samaveta*—assembled.

(21) All glories to the assembled devotees.

(22) *gaura*—(of) Lord Caitanya; *prema*—(of) love; *ānande*—in the ecstacy; *hari*—He who takes away (the distress of His devotees); *bol*—chant.

Chant the names Hari! Hari! in the ecstacy of love for Lord Caitanya.

Śrī Śrī Śikṣāṣṭaka

Lord Caitanya Mahāprabhu instructed His disciples to write books on the science of Kṛṣṇa, a task which His followers have continued to carry out to the present day. The elaborations and expositions on the philosophy taught by Lord Caitanya are, in fact the most voluminous, exacting, and consistent, due to the system of disciplic succession. Although Lord Caitanya was widely renowned as a scholar in His youth, He left only eight verses, called Śikṣāṣṭaka. These eight verses clearly reveal His mission and precepts. These verses are described more elaborately in the *Śrī Caitanya-caritāmṛta, Antya-līlā*, Chapter 20.

(1)

ceto-darpaṇa-mārjanaṁ
bhava-mahā-dāvāgni-nirvāpaṇaṁ
śreyaḥ-kairava-candrikā-vitaraṇaṁ
vidyā-vadhu-jīvanam
ānandāmbudhi-vardhanaṁ
prati-padaṁ pūrṇāmṛtāsvādanaṁ
sarvātma-snapanaṁ paraṁ
vijayate śrī-kṛṣṇa-saṅkīrtanam

(2)

nāmnām akāri bahudhā nija-sarva-śaktis
tatrārpitā niyamitaḥ smaraṇe na kālaḥ
etādṛśī tava kṛpā bhagavan mamāpi
durdaivam īdṛśam ihājani nānurāgaḥ

(3)

tṛṇād api sunīcena
taror api sahiṣṇunā
amāninā mānadena
kīrtanīyaḥ sadā hariḥ

(4)

na dhanaṁ na janaṁ na sundarīṁ
kavitāṁ vā jagad-īśa kāmaye
mama janmani janmanīśvare
bhavatād bhaktir ahaituki tvayi

(5)

ayi nanda-tanuja kiṅkaraṁ
patitaṁ māṁ viṣame bhavāmbudhau
kṛpayā tava pāda-paṅkaja-
sthita-dhūlī-sadṛśaṁ vicintaya

(6)

nayanaṁ galad-aśru-dhārayā
vadanaṁ gadgada-ruddhayā girā
pulakair nicitaṁ vapuḥ kadā
tava nāma-grahaṇe bhaviṣyati

(7)

yugāyitaṁ nimeṣeṇa
cakṣuṣā prāvṛṣāyitam
śūnyāyitaṁ jagat sarvaṁ
govinda-viraheṇa me

(8)

āśliṣya vā pāda-ratāṁ pinaṣṭu mām
adarśanān marma-hatāṁ karotu vā
yathā tathā vā vidadhātu lampaṭo
mat-prāṇa-nāthas tu sa eva nāparaḥ

(1) *cetaḥ*—of the heart; *darpaṇa*—the mirror; *mārjanam*—cleansing; *bhava*—of material existence; *mahā-dāva-agni*—the blazing forest fire; *nirvāpaṇam*—extinguishing; *śreyaḥ*—of good fortune; *kairava*—the white lotus; *candrikā*—the moonshine; *vitaraṇam*—spreading; *vidyā*—of all education; *vadhu*—wife; *jīvanam*—the life; *ānanda*—of bliss; *ambudhi*—the ocean; *vardhanam*—increasing; *prati-padam*—at every step; *pūrṇa-amṛta*—of the full nectar; *āsvādanam*—giving a taste; *sarva*—for everyone; *ātma-snapanam*—bathing of the self; *param*—transcendental; *vijayate*—let there be victory; *śrī-kṛṣṇa-saṅkīrtanam*—for the congregational chanting of the holy name of Kṛṣṇa.

Let there be all victory for the chanting of the holy name of Lord Kṛṣṇa, which can cleanse the mirror of the heart and stop the miseries of the blazing fire of material existence. That chanting is the waxing moon that spreads the white lotus of good fortune for all living entities. It is the life and soul of all education. The chanting of the holy name of Kṛṣṇa expands the blissful ocean of transcendental life. It gives a cooling effect to everyone and enables one to taste full nectar at every step.

(2) *nāmnām*—of the holy names of the Lord; *akāri* —manifested; *bahudhā*—various kinds; *nija-sarva-śaktiḥ*—all kinds of personal potencies; *tatra*—in that; *arpitā*—bestowed; *niyamitaḥ*—restricted; *smaraṇe*—in remembering; *na*—not; *kālaḥ*—consideration of time; *etādṛśī*—so much; *tava*—Your; *kṛpā*—mercy; *bhagavan*—O Lord; *mama*—My; *api*—although; *durdaivam*—misfortune; *īdṛśam*—such; *iha*—in this (the holy name); *ajani*—was born; *na*—not; *anurāgaḥ*—attachment.

My Lord, O Supreme Personality of Godhead, in Your holy name there is all good fortune for the living entity, and therefore You have many names, such as Kṛṣṇa and Govinda, by which You expand Yourself. You have invested all Your potencies in those names, and there are no hard and fast rules for remembering them. My dear Lord, although You bestow such mercy upon the fallen, conditioned souls by liberally teaching Your holy names, I am so unfortunate that I commit offenses while chanting the holy name, and therefore I do not achieve attachment for chanting.

(3) *tṛṇāt api*—than downtrodden grass; *su-nīcena* —being lower; *taroḥ*—than tree; *iva*—like; *sahiṣṇunā*—with tolerance; *amāninā*—without being puffed up by false pride; *māna-dena*—

giving respect to all; *kīrtanīyaḥ*—to be chanted; *sadā*—always; *hariḥ*—the holy name of the Lord.

One who thinks himself lower than the grass, who is more tolerant than a tree, and who does not expect personal honor but is always prepared to give all respect to others can very easily always chant the holy name of the Lord.

(4) *na*—not; *dhanam*—riches; *na*—not; *janam*—followers; *na*—not; *sundarīm*—a very beautiful woman; *kavitām*—fruitive activities described in flowery language; *vā*—or; *jagat-īśa*—O Lord of the universe; *kāmaye*—I desire; *mama*—My; *janmani janmani*—in birth after birth; *īśvare*—unto the Supreme Personality of Godhead; *bhavatāt*—let there be; *bhaktiḥ*—devotional service; *ahaitukī*—with no motives; *tvayi*—unto You.

O Lord of the universe, I do not desire material wealth, materialistic followers, a beautiful wife or fruitive activities described in flowery language. All I want, life after life, is unmotivated devotional service to You.

(5) *ayi*—O My Lord; *nanda-tanuja*—the son of Nanda Mahārāja, Kṛṣṇa; *kiṅkaram*—the servant; *patitam*—fallen; *mām*—Me; *viṣame*—horrible;

bhava-ambudhau—in the ocean of nescience; *kṛpayā*—by causeless mercy; *tava*—Your; *pāda-paṅkaja*—lotus feet; *sthita*—situated at; *dhūlī-sadṛśam*—like a particle of dust; *vicintaya*—kindly consider.

O My Lord, O Kṛṣṇa, son of Mahārāja Nanda, I am Your eternal servant, but because of My own fruitive acts I have fallen into this horrible ocean of nescience. Now please be causelessly merciful to Me. Consider Me a particle of dust at your lotus feet.

(6) *nayanam*—the eyes; *galat-aśru-dharayā*—by streams of tears running down; *vadanam*—mouth; *gadgada*—faltering; *ruddhayā*—choked up; *girā*—with words; *pulakaiḥ*—with erection of the hairs due to transcendental happiness; *nicitam*—covered; *vapuḥ*—the body; *kadā*—when; *tava*—Your; *nāma-grahaṇe*—in chanting the name; *bhaviṣyati*—will be.

My dear Lord, when will My eyes be beautified by filling with tears that constantly glide down as I chant Your holy name? When will my voice falter and all the hairs on My body stand erect in transcendental happiness as I chant Your holy name?

(7) *yugāyitam*—appearing like a great millenium; *nimeṣeṇa*—by a moment; *cakṣuṣā*—from the eyes; *prāvṛṣāyitam*—tears falling like torrents of rain; *śūnyāyitam*—appearing void; *jagat*—the world; *sarvam*—all; *govinda*—from Lord Govinda, Kṛṣṇa; *viraheṇa me*—by My (Lord Caitanya's) separation.

My Lord Govinda, because of separation from You, I consider even a moment a great millennium. Tears flow from my eyes like torrents of rain, and I can see the entire world as void.

(8) *āśliṣya*—embracing with great pleasure; *vā*—or; *pāda-ratām*—who have fallen at the lotus feet; *pinaṣṭu*—let Him trample; *mām*—Me; *adarśanāt*—by not being visible; *marma-hatām*—broken-hearted; *karotu*—let Him make; *vā*—or; *yathā*—as (He likes); *tathā*—so; *vā*—or; *vidadhātu*—let Him do; *lampaṭaḥ*—a debauchee, who mixes with other women; *mat-prāna-nāthaḥ*—the Lord of My life; *tu*—but; *saḥ*—He; *eva*—only; *na aparaḥ*—not anyone else.

Let Kṛṣṇa tightly embrace this maidservant who has fallen at His lotus feet, or let Him trample Me or break My heart by never being visible to Me. He is a debauchee, after all, and can do whatever He likes, but He is still no other than the worshipable Lord of My heart.

Honoring Prasāda

You should be clean when you take your meal, having washed your hands and mouth. You should eat in a clean, spacious, peaceful place. Do not eat before bathing or until the food from the previous meal has been digested.

Before beginning a meal, you should glorify the Lord's *prasāda* by chanting the following prayers:

mahā-prasāde govinde
nāma-brahmaṇi vaiṣṇave
svalpa-puṇya-vatāṁ rājan
viśvāso naiva jāyate

mahā-prasāde—in *mahā-prasāda*; *govinde*—in Śrī Govinda; *nāma-brahmaṇi*—in the holy name; *vaiṣṇave*—in the Vaiṣṇavas; *su-alpa-puṇya-vatām*—for those with very little pious credit; *rājan*—O king; *viśvāsaḥ*—faith; *na*—never; *eva*—certainly; *jāyate*—arises.

O king, for those with little pious credit, faith in *mahā-prasāda,* Śrī Govinda, the holy name, and Vaiṣṇavas never arises.

—*Mahābhārata*

Prasāda-sevāya

Honoring Prasāda in the Mood of Service

by Śrīla Bhaktivinoda Ṭhākura

(1)

bhāi-re!
śarīra abidyā-jāl, joḍendriya tāhe kāl,
jīve phele viṣaya-sāgore
tā'ra madhye jihwā ati, lobhamoy sudurmati,
tā'ke jetā kaṭhina saṁsāre

(2)

kṛṣṇa baṛo doyāmoy, koribāre jihwā jay,
swa-prasād-anna dilo bhāi
sei annāmṛta pāo, rādhā-kṛṣṇa-guṇa gāo,
preme ḍāko caitanya-nitāi

WORD MEANINGS AND TRANSLATIONS

(1) *bhāi-re*—O brothers! *śarīra*—(this material) body; *abidyā*—(of) ignorance; *jāl*—a network; *joḍa-indriya*—the dull material senses; *tāhe*—in them; *kāl*—death; *jīve*—the soul; *phele*—throw; *viṣaya*—(of) material sense enjoyment; *sāgore*—into the ocean; *tā'ra mdhye*—among them (the senses); *jihwā*—the tongue; *ati*—very much; *lobhamoy*—voracious; *sudurmati*—of a very bad

disposition, uncontrollable; *tā'ke*—it (the tongue); *jetā*—to conquer; *kaṭhina*—very difficult; *saṁsāre*—in (this) world.

O brothers! This material body is a network of ignorance, and the senses are one's deadly enemies, for they throw the soul into this ocean of material sense enjoyment. Among those senses the tongue is most voracious and uncontrollable; it is very difficult to conquer the tongue in this world.

(2) *kṛṣṇa*—Lord Kṛṣṇa; *baṛo*—very; *doyāmoy*—merciful; *koribāre*—for doing; *jihwā*—(over) the tongue; *jay*—victory; *swa*—His own; *prasād*—mercy; *anna*—food; *dilā*—has given; *bhāi*—O brothers! *sei*—that; *anna-amṛta*—nectarean food; *pāo*—please accept; *rādhā-kṛṣṇa*—of Rādhā and Kṛṣṇa; *guṇa*—the glories; *gāo*—sing; *preme*—in love; *ḍāko*—call out; *caitanya-nitāi*—Caitanya! Nitāi!

O brothers! Lord Kṛṣṇa is very merciful and has given us the remnants of His own food just to control the tongue. Now please accept that nectarean *kṛṣṇa-prasāda* and sing the glories of Their Lordships Śrī Śrī Rādhā and Kṛṣṇa, and in love call out, "Caitanya! Nitāi!"

Śrī Nāma-kīrtana

Chanting of the Holy Names

by Śrīla Bhaktivinoda Ṭhākura

(1)

yaśomatī-nandana, braja-baro-nāgara,
gokula-rañjana kāna
gopī-parāṇa-dhana, madana-manohara,
kāliya-damana-vidhāna

(2)

amala harinām amiya-vilāsā
vipina-purandara, navīna nāgara-baro,
baṁśī-badana suvāsā

(3)

braja-jana-pālana, asura-kula-nāśana,
nanda-godhana-rākhowālā
govinda mādhava, navanīta-taskara,
sundara nanda-gopālā

(4)

jāmuna-taṭa-cara, gopī-basana-hara,
rāsa-rasika, kṛpāmoya
śrī-rādhā-vallabha, bṛndābana-naṭabara,
bhakativinod-āśraya

(1) *yaśomatī*—(of) Mother Yaśodā; *nanda*—the beloved son; *braja*—(of) the land of Vraja; *baro*—the best; *nāgara*—inhabitant; *gokula*—(of the people of) Gokula; *rañjana*—the delight; *kāna*—a nickname of Kṛṣṇa; *gopī*—(of) the *gopīs*; *parāṇa*—(of) the lives; *dhana*—the wealth; *madana*—(of) Cupid, the god of love; *manohara*—attracter; *kāliya*—(of) the Kāliya serpent; *damana*—(of) the punishment; *vidhāna*—the doer.

Lord Kṛṣṇa is the beloved son of mother Yaśodā; the transcendental lover in the land of Vraja; the delight of Gokula; Kāna [a nickname of Kṛṣṇa]; the wealth of the lives of the *gopīs*. He steals the mind of even Cupid and punishes the Kāliya serpent.

(2) *amala*—pure; *harināma*—holy names of Lord Hari; *amiya*—nectarean; *vilāsa*—pastimes; *vipina*—(of) the forest (Vṛndāvana); *purandara*—the Lord; *navīna*—ever-youthful; *nāgara*—(of) lovers; *baro*—the best; *vaṁśī*—flute; *vadana*—(at His) mouth; *suvāsā*—the wearer of beautiful clothing.

These pure, holy names of Lord Hari are full of sweet, nectarean pastimes. Kṛṣṇa is the Lord of Vṛndāvana. He is ever-youthful and is the best of lovers. He is always playing on a flute, and He is an excellent dresser.

(3) *braja*—(of) the land of Vraja; *jana*—(of) the inhabitants; *pālana*—the protector; *asura*—(of) the demons; *kula*—(of) the dynasties; *nāśana*—the destroyer; *nanda*—(of) Nanda Mahārāja; *godhana* —(of) the multitude of cows; *rākhowālā*—the keeper and tender; *govinda*—the giver of pleasure to the cows, land and spiritual senses; *mādhava*—the husband of the goddess of fortune; *navanīta*—butter; *taskara*—thief; *sundara*—beautiful; *nanda* —(of) Nanda Mahārāja; *gopālā*—protector of the cows, cowherd boy.

Kṛṣṇa is the protector of the inhabitants of Vraja; the destroyer of various demoniac dynasties; the keeper and tender of Nanda Mahārāja's cows; the giver of pleasure to the cows, land and spiritual senses; the husband of the goddess of fortune; the butter thief; and the beautiful cowherd boy of Nanda Mahārāja.

(4) *jāmuna*—of the River Yamunā; *taṭa*—(along) the banks; *cara*—wandering; *gopī*—(of) the *gopīs*; *basana*—(of) the garments; *hara*—the stealer; *rāsa*—(of) the *rāsa* dance; *rasika*—the relisher of the mellows; *kṛpāmoya*—very merciful; *śrī-rādhā*—(of) Śrīmatī Rādhārāṇī; *vallabha*—the

lover and beloved; *bṛndābana*—(of) Vṛndāvana; *naṭabara*—the great dancer; *bhakativinod*—(of) Bhaktivinoda Ṭhākura; *āśraya*—the shelter.

Kṛṣṇa wanders along the banks of the River Yamunā. He stole the garments of the young damsels of Vraja who were bathing there. He delights in the mellows of the *rāsa* dance. He is very merciful; the lover and beloved of Śrīmatī Rādhārāṇī; the great dancer of Vṛndāvana; and the shelter and only refuge of Ṭhākura Bhaktivinoda.

Sāvaraṇa-śrī-gaura-pāda-padme Prārthanā

A prayer to the Lotus Feet of Śrī Gaurāṅga
by Śrīḷa Narottama dāsa Ṭhākura

(1)

śrī-kṛṣṇa-caitanya prabhu doyā koro more
tomā binā ke doyālu jagat-saṁsāre

(2)

patita-pāvana-hetu tava avatāra
mo sama patita prabhu nā pāibe āra

(3)

hā hā prabhu nityānanda, premānanda sukhī
kṛpābalokana koro āmi boṛo duḥkhī

(4)

doyā koro sītā-pati adwaita gosāi
tava kṛpā-bale pāi caitanya-nitāi

(5)

hā hā swarūp, sanātana, rūpa, raghunātha
bhaṭṭa-juga, śrī-jīva hā prabhu lokanātha

(6)

doyā koro śrī-ācārya prabhu śrīnivāsa
rāmacandra-saṅga māge narottama-dāsa

WORD MEANINGS AND TRANSLATIONS

(title) *sāvaraṇa*—protective; *śri-gaura*—(of) Śrī Gaurāṅga; *pāda-padme*—to the lotus feet; *prārthanā*—a prayer.

A prayer to the Lotus Feet of Śrī Gaurāṅga

(1) *śrī-kṛṣṇa-caitanya prabhu*—O my Lord Śrī Kṛṣna Caitanya! *doyā koro*—please be merciful; *more*—to me; *tomā binā*—other than you; *ke*—who? *dayālu*—merciful; *jagat-saṁsāre*—in this material world.

O my Lord, Śrī Kṛṣṇa Caitanya, please be merciful to me, because other than You who is merciful in this material world?

(2) *patita*—(of) the fallen; *pāvana*—the deliverance; *hetu*—the purpose; *tava*—Your; *avatāra*—descent, incarnation; *mo sama*—as me; *patita*—(as) fallen; *prabhu*—O Lord; *nā pāibe*—You will not find; *āra*—another.

The reason for your descent into this material world is to deliver the fallen, conditioned souls, but You will not find anyone more fallen than me.

(3) *hā hā*—O; *prabhu*—Lord; *nityānanda*—Nityānanda; *prema-ānanda*—(in) the bliss of divine love; *sukhī*—happy; *kṛpā*—(of) mercy; *abalokana*—glance; *koro*—please cast; *āmi*—I; *boṛo*—very; *duḥkhī*—unhappy.

O Lord Nityānanda, You are always happy in the bliss of divine love; but I am very unhappy, therefore please cast Your merciful glance upon me.

(4) *doyā koro*—please be merciful; *sītā-pati*—husband of Sītā; *adwaita gosāi*—Adwaita Prabhu; *tava*—Your; *kṛpā*—(of) mercy; *bale*—by the strength; *pāi*—one can attain; *caitanya-nitāi*—(the mercy of) Lord Caitanya and Lord Nityānanda.

My dear Adwaita Prabhu, husband of Sītā, please be kind to me. By the strength of Your mercy one can attain the mercy of Lord Caitanya and Lord Nityānanda.

(5) *hā hā*—O; *swarūp*—Swarūpa Dāmodara, the personal secretary of Lord Caitanya; *sanātana*—Sanātana Goswāmī; *rūpa*—Śrīla Rūpa Goswāmī; *raghunātha*—Śrīla Raghunātha dāsa Goswāmī; *bhaṭṭa-juga*—the two Bhaṭṭas, Śrīla Raghunātha Bhaṭṭa Goswāmī and Śrīla Gopāla Bhaṭṭa Goswāmī; *śrī-jīva*—Śrīla Jīva Goswāmī; *hā prabhu*—O master! *lokanātha*—Śrīla Lokanātha Goswāmī, the initiating guru of Śrīla Narottama dāsa Ṭhākura.

O Swarūpa Dāmodara, Sanātana Goswāmī, Rūpa Goswāmī, Raghunātha dāsa Goswāmī, Raghunātha Bhaṭṭa Goswāmī, Gopāla Bhaṭṭa Goswāmī, Jīva Goswāmī and Lokanātha Goswāmī, please be merciful to me.

(6) *doyā koro*—please be merciful; *śrī-ācārya prabhu śrīnivāsa*—Śrīla Śrīnivāsācārya Prabhu; *rāmacandra*—(of) Rāmacandra Kavirāja, a disciple of Śrīnivāsācārya and personal friend of Narottama dāsa; *saṅga*—the association; *māge*—prays for; *narottama-dāsa*—Śrīla Narottama dāsa Ṭhākura.

O Śrīnivāsācārya Prabhu, please be merciful to me. Narottama dāsa Ṭhākura prays for the association of his personal friend, Śrī Rāmacandra Kavirāja.

Nāma-saṅkīrtana

by Śrīla Narottama dāsa Ṭhākura

(1)

(hari) haraye namaḥ kṛṣṇa yādavāya namaḥ
yādavāya mādhavāya keśavāya namaḥ

(2)

gopāla govinda rāma śrī-madhusūdana
giridhārī gopīnātha madana-mohana

(3)

śrī-caitanya-nityānanda śrī-adwaita-sītā
hari guru vaiṣṇava bhāgavata gītā

(4)

śrī-rūpa sanātana bhaṭṭa-raghunāth
śrī-jīva gopāla-bhaṭṭa dāsa-raghunāth

(5)

ei chay gosāir kori caraṇa vandan
jāhā hoite bighna-nāś abhīṣṭa-pūraṇ

(6)

ei chay gosāi jār——mui tār dās
tāṅ-sabāra pada-reṇu mora pañca-grās

(7)

tāndera caraṇa-sebi bhakta-sane bās
janame janame hoy ei abhilāṣ

(8)

ei chay gosāi jabe braje koilā bās
rādha-kṛṣṇa-nitya-līlā korilā prakāś

(9)

ānande bolo hari bhaja bṛndāban
śrī-guru-vaiṣṇaba-pade majāiya man

(10)

śrī-guru-vaiṣṇaba-pāda-padma kori āś
nāma-saṅkīrtana kohe narottama-dās

WORD MEANINGS AND TRANSLATIONS

(1) *hari*—O Lord Hari; *haraye*—unto Lord Hari; *namaḥ*—I offer my obeisances; *kṛṣṇa*—O Lord Kṛṣṇa; *yādavāya*—unto Yādava (the descendant of King Yadu); *namaḥ*—I offer my obeisances; *yādavāya*—unto Yādava; *mādhavāya*—unto Mādhava (the husband of the goddess of fortune);

keśavāya—unto Keśava (one having fine hair); *namaḥ*—I offer my obeisances.

O Lord Hari, O Lord Kṛṣṇa, I offer my obeisances to You, who are known as Yādava, Hari, Mādhava and Keśava.

(2) *gopāla*—the protector of the cows; *govinda*—the giver of pleasure to the cows, land and spiritual senses; *rāma*—one who enjoys supreme transcendental pleasure; *śrī-madhusūdana*—the killer of the demon Madhu; *giridhārī*—the lifter of the (Govardhana) Hill; *gopīnātha*—the Lord of the *gopīs*; *madana-mohana*—the attractor of Cupid.

O Gopāla, Govinda, Rāma, Śrī Mudhusūdana, Giridhārī, Gopīnātha, Madana-mohana!

(3) *śrī-caitanya-nityānanda*—Śrī Caitanya and Nityānanda; *śri-adwaita-sītā*—Śrī Adwaita Ācārya and His consort, Sītā Ṭhākurāṇī; *hari*—Lord Hari; *guru*—the spiritual master; *vaiṣṇaba*—the Vaiṣṇavas; *bhāgavata*—the *Śrīmad-Bhāgavatam*; *gītā*—the *Bhagavad-gītā*.

All glories to Śrī Caitanya and Nityānanda. All glories to Śrī Advaita Ācārya and His consort, Sītā Ṭhākurāṇī. All glories to Lord Hari, the spiritual master, the Vaiṣṇavas, the *Śrīmad-Bhāgavatam* and the *Bhagavad-gītā.*

(4) *śrī-rūpa*—Śrī Rūpa Goswāmī; *sanātana*—Sanātana Goswāmī; *bhaṭṭa-raghunātha*—Raghunātha Bhaṭṭa Goswāmī; *śrī-jīva*—Śrī Jīva Goswāmī; *gopāla-bhaṭṭa*—Gopāla Bhaṭṭa Goswāmī; *dāsa-raghunāth*—Raghunātha dāsa Goswāmī.

All glories to Śrī Rūpa Goswāmī, Sanātana Goswāmī, Raghunātha Bhaṭṭa Goswāmī, Śrī Jīva Goswāmī, Gopāla Bhaṭṭa Goswāmī, and Raghunātha dāsa Goswāmī.

(5) *ei*—these; *chay*—six; *gosāir*—of (the) Goswāmīs; *kori*—I offer; *caraṇa*—(to) the feet; *vandan*—(my) obeisances; *jāhā hoite*—from which; *bighna*—(of) obstacles; *nāś*—the destruction; *abhīṣṭa*—spiritual desires; *pūraṇ*—fulfilled.

I offer my obeisances to the feet of these six Goswāmīs. By offering them my obeisances all obstacles to devotion are destroyed and all spiritual desires are fulfilled.

(6) *ei*—these; *chay*—six; *gosāi*—Goswāmīs; *jār*—(the servant) of whom; *mui*—I (am); *tār*—his; *dās*—servant; *tāṅ-sabāra*—of all of them; *pada*—

of (their holy) feet; *reṇu*—the dust; *mora*—my; *pañca* —five kinds; *grās*—(of) food.

I am the servant of that person who is a servant of these six Goswāmīs. The dust of their holy feet is my five kinds of food.

(7) *tāndera*—their; *caraṇa*—feet; *sebi*—who serve; *bhakta*—the devotees; *sane*—with; *bās*—residence; *janame janame*—birth after birth; *hoy*—is; *ei*—this; *abhilāṣ*—(my) desire.

This is my desire, that birth after birth I may live with those devotees who serve the lotus feet of these six Goswāmīs.

(8) *ei*—these; *chay*—six; *gosāi*—Goswāmīs; *jabe* —when; *braje*—in Vraja; *koilā*—made; *bās*—residence; *rādhā-kṛṣṇa*—of Rādhā and Kṛṣṇa; *nitya*—eternal; *līlā*—pastimes; *korilā*—made; *prakāś*—clearly visible.

When these six Goswāmīs lived in Vraja they revealed and explained the eternal pastimes of Rādhā and Kṛṣṇa.

(9) *ānande*—in ecstacy; *bolo*—chant; *hari*—the names of Lord Hari; *bhaja*—worship; *bṛndāban*—Vṛndāvana; *śrī-guru-vaiṣṇaba*—of the spiritual

master and the Vaiṣṇavas; *pade*—on the lotus feet; *majāiya*—absorbing in meditation; *man*—the mind.

Absorbing your mind in meditation upon the divine feet of the spiritual master and the holy Vaiṣṇavas, chant the names of Lord Hari in ecstasy, and worship the transcendental realm of Vṛndāvana.

(10) *śrī-guru-vaiṣṇaba*—of the spiritual master and the Vaiṣṇavas; *pāda*—the feet; *padma*—lotus; *kori āś*—desiring; *nāma-saṅkīrtana*—the *saṅkītana* of the holy name; *kohe*—sings; *narottama-dās*—Narottama dāsa.

Desiring the lotus feet of Śrī Guru and the Vaiṣṇavas, Narottama dāsa sings the *saṅkīrtana* of the holy name.

Sapārṣada-bhagavad-viraha-janita-vilāpa

Lamentation Due to Separation from the Lord and His Associates
by Śrīla Narottama dāsa Ṭhākura

Śrīla Prabhupāda wanted this song to be sung on the disappearance days of great Vaiṣṇavas.

(1)

je ānilo prema-dhana koruṇā pracur
heno prabhu kothā gelā ācārya-ṭhākur

(2)

kāhā mora swarūp rūpa kāhā sanātan
kāhā dāsa raghunātha patita-pāvan

(3)

kāhā mora bhaṭṭa-juga kāhā kavirāj
eka-kāle kothā gelā gorā naṭa-rāj

(4)

pāṣāṇe kuṭibo māthā anale pāśibo
gaurāṅga guṇera nidhi kothā gele pābo

(5)

se-saba saṅgīra saṅge je koilo bilās
se-saṅga nā pāiyā kānde narottama dās

(title) *sapārṣada*—along with (His) associates; *bhagavad*—(from) the Lord; *viraha*—separation; *janita*—due to; *vilāpa*—lamentation .

Lamentation Due to Separation from the Lord and His Associates

(1) *je ānilo*—he who brought; *prema-dhana*—the treasure of love (of God); *koruṇā*—compassion; *pracur*—unlimited; *heno prabhu*—such a master; *kothā*—where; *gelā*—has gone; *ācārya-ṭhākur*—Śrīla Śrīnivācārya.

He who brought the treasure of divine love and who was filled with unlimited compassion and mercy—where has such a personality as Śrīnivāsācārya gone?

(2) *kāhā*—where (is); *mora*—my; *swarūp*—Swarūpa Dāmodara Goswāmī; *rūpa*—Rūpa Goswāmī; *kāhā*—where (is); *sanātan*—Sanātana Goswāmī; *kāhā*—where (is); *dāsa raghunātha*—Raghunātha Dāsa Goswāmī; *patita-pāvan*—the saviour of the fallen souls.

Where are my Swarūpa Dāmodara and Rūpa Goswāmī? Where is Sanātana? Where is Raghunātha Dāsa, the saviour of the fallen?

(3) *kāhā*—where (are); *mora*—my; *bhaṭṭa-juga*—the two Bhaṭṭas (Raghunātha Bhaṭṭa Goswāmī and Gopāla Bhaṭṭa Goswāmi); *kāhā*—where (is); *kavirāj*—Kṛṣṇadāsa Kavirāja Goswāmī; *eka-kāle*—suddenly; *kothā*—where; *gelā*—did go; *gorā*—Lord Gaurāṅga; *naṭa-rāj*—the great dancer.

Where are my Raghunātha Bhaṭṭa and Gopāla Bhaṭṭa and where is Kṛṣṇadāsa Kavirāja? Where did Lord Gaurāṅga, the great dancer, suddenly go?

(4) *pāṣāṇe*—upon a stone; *kuṭibo*—I will smash; *māthā*—(my) head; *anale*—into fire; *pāśibo*—I will enter; *gaurāṅga*—Lord Gaurāṅga; *guṇera*—of (all wonderful) qualities; *nidhi*—the ocean; *kothā*—where; *gele*—going; *pābo*—I will find.

I will smash my head upon a stone and will enter into fire. Where will I find Lord Gaurāṅga, the ocean of all wonderful qualities?

(5) *se-saba*—all these; *saṅgīra*—of associates; *saṅge*—accompanied by; *je*—He who; *koilo bilās*—performed pastimes; *se-saṅga*—that

association; *nā*—not; *pāiyā*—obtaining; *kānde*—is weeping; *narottama dās*—Narottama dāsa.

Being unable to obtain the association of Lord Gaurāṅga, accompanied by all of these devotees in whose association He performed His pastimes, Narottama dāsa simply weeps.

Iṣṭa-deve Vijñapti

Prayer to One's Beloved Lord
by Śrīla Narottama dāsa Ṭhākura

During September of 1969 in England Śrīla Prabhupāda said that this was his favorite bhajan. (*Śrīla Prabhupāda Līlāmṛta*, Vol. 4, p. 48)

(1)
hari hari! bifale janama goṅāinu
manuṣya-janama pāiyā, rādhā-kṛṣṇa nā bhajiyā,
jāniyā śuniyā biṣa khāinu

(2)
golokera prema-dhana, hari-nāma-saṅkīrtana,
rati nā janmilo kene tāy
saṁsāra-biṣānale, dibā-niśi hiyā jwale,
jurāite nā koinu upāy

(3)

brajendra-nandana jei, śacī-suta hoilo sei,
balarāma hoilo nitāi
dīna-hīna jata chilo, hari-nāme uddhārilo,
tāra sākṣī jagāi mādhāi

(4)

hā hā prabhu nanda-suta, vṛṣabhānu-sutā-juta,
koruṇā karoho ei-bāro
narottama-dāsa koy, nā ṭheliho rāṅgā pāy,
tomā bine ke āche āmāra

WORD MEANINGS AND TRANSLATIONS

(title) *iṣṭa*—dear, worshipable; *deve*—to the Lord; *vijñapti*—prayer, entreaty.

(1) *hari hari*—O Lord Hari; *bifale*—unsuccessfully; *janama*—human form of life; *goṅāinu*—I have spent; *manuṣya-janama*—human birth; *pāiyā*—having obtained; *rādhā-kṛṣṇa*—Rādhā and Kṛṣṇa; *nā*—not; *bhajiyā*—worshipping; *jāniyā*—knowingly; *śuniyā*—having heard; *biṣa*—poison; *khāinu*—I have drunk.

O Lord Hari, I have spent my life uselessly. Having obtained a human birth and having not worshiped Rādhā and Kṛṣṇa, I have knowingly drunk poison.

(2) *golokera*—of Goloka Vṛndāvana; *prema-dhana*—the treasure of (divine) love; *hari-nāma-saṅkīrtana*—the congregational chanting of Lord Hari's holy names; *rati*—(my) attraction; *nā janmilo*—did not come about; *kene*—why? *tāy*—for that; *saṁsāra*—(of) material existence; *biṣa-anale*—from the fire of the poison; *dibā-niśi*—day and night; *hiyā*—(my) heart; *jwale*—burns; *jurāite*—to relieve (it); *nā koinu upāy*—I have not taken the means.

The treasure of divine love in Goloka Vṛndāvana has descended as the congregational chanting of Lord Hari's holy names. Why did my attraction for that chanting never come about? Day and night my heart burns from the fire of the poison of material existence, and I have not taken the means to relieve it.

(3) *brajendra-nandana*—the son of the king of Braja; *jei*—He who; *śacī-suta*—the son of Śacī; *hoilo*—became; *sei*—He; *balarāma*—Balarāma; *hoilo*—became; *nitāi*—Lord Nityānanda; *dīna*—poor; *hīna*—low born; *jata*—as many; *chilo*—as there were; *hari-nāme*—by the chanting of the holy names; *uddhārilo*—were delivered; *tāra*—of this; *sākṣī*—evidence; *jagāi mādhāi*—(the two sinners) Jagāi and Mādhāi.

Lord Kṛṣṇa, who is the son of the King of Vraja, became the son of Śacī (Lord Caitanya), and Balarāma became Nitāi. All those souls who were lowly and wretched were delivered by the chanting of the holy names. The two sinners Jagāi and Mādhāi are evidence of this.

(4) *hā hā prabhu*—O Lord; *nanda-suta*—the son of Nanda; *vṛṣabhānu-sutā*—the daughter of Vṛṣabhānu; *juta*—accompanied by; *koruṇā karoho*—please be merciful (to me); *ei-bāro*—at this time; *narottama-dāsa*—Narottama dāsa; *koy*—says; *nā ṭheliho*—please don't push (me) away; *rāṅgā pāy*—(from) Your reddish lotus feet; *tomā bine*—except for You; *ke āche*—who else is? *āmāra*—mine.

O Lord Kṛṣṇa, son of Nanda, acompanied by the daughter of Vṛṣabhānu, please be merciful to me at this time. Narottama dāsa says, "O Lord, please do not push me away from Your reddish lotus feet, for except for You who is my beloved?"

Śrī Dāmodarāṣṭaka

(found in the *Padma Purāṇa* of Kṛṣṇa Dvaipāyana Vyāsa, spoken by Satyavrata Muni in a conversation with Nārada Muni and Śaunaka Ṛṣi)

"In the month of Kārtik one should worship Lord Dāmodara and daily recite the prayer known as *Dāmodāraṣṭaka,* which has been spoken by the sage Satyavrata and which attracts Lord Dāmodara."

(*Śrī Hari-bhakti-vilāsa* 2.16.198)

(1)

namāmīśvaraṁ sac-cid-ānanda-rūpaṁ
lasat-kuṇḍalaṁ gokule bhrājamānam
yaśodā-bhiyolūkhalād dhāvamānaṁ
parāmṛṣṭam atyantato drutya gopyā

(2)

rudantaṁ muhur netra-yugmaṁ mṛjantaṁ
karāmbhoja-yugmena sātaṅka-netram
muhuḥ śvāsa-kampa-trirekhāṅka-kaṇṭha-
sthita-graivaṁ dāmodaraṁ bhakti-baddham

(3)

itīdṛk sva-līlābhir ānanda-kuṇḍe
sva-ghoṣaṁ nimajjantam ākhyāpayantam
tadīyeśita-jñeṣu bhaktair jitatvaṁ
punaḥ prematas taṁ śatāvṛtti vande

(4)

varaṁ deva mokṣaṁ na mokṣāvadhiṁ vā
na cānyaṁ vṛṇe 'haṁ vareśād apīha
idaṁ te vapur nātha gopāla-bālaṁ
sadā me manasy āvirāstāṁ kim anyaiḥ

(5)

idaṁ te mukhāmbhojam atyanta-nīlair
vṛtaṁ kuntalaiḥ snigdha-raktaiś ca gopyā
muhuś cumbitaṁ bimba-raktādharaṁ me
manasy āvirāstām alaṁ lakṣa-lābhaiḥ

(6)

namo deva dāmodarānanta viṣṇo
prasīda prabho duḥkha-jālābdhi-magnam
kṛpā-dṛṣṭi-vṛṣṭyāti-dīnaṁ batānu-
gṛhāṇeśa mām ajñam edhy akṣi-dṛśyaḥ

(7)

kuverātmajau baddha-mūrtyaiva yadvat
tvayā mocitau bhakti-bhājau kṛtau ca
tathā prema-bhaktiṁ svakāṁ me prayaccha
na mokṣe graho me 'sti dāmodareha

(8)

namas te 'stu dāmne sphurad-dīpti-dhāmne
tvadīyodarāyātha viśvasya dhāmne
namo rādhikāyai tvadīya- priyāyai
namo 'nanta-līlāya devāya tubhyam

WORD MEANINGS AND TRANSLATIONS

(1) *namāmi*—I offer my humble obeisances; *īśvaram*—to the Lord; *sat cit ānanda*—eternal, full of knowledge and bliss; *rūpam*—(whose) form; *lasat*—glistening and swinging to and fro; *kuṇḍalam*—(whose) earrings; *gokule*—in Gokula; *bhrājamānam*—brilliantly; *yaśodā*—of Mother Yaśodā; *bhiya*—out of fear; *ulūkhalāt*—from the grinding mortar; *dhāvamānam*—fleeing; *parāmṛṣṭam*—caught; *atyantataḥ*—ultimately; *drutya*—quickly running; *gopyā*—by the gopī (Yaśodā).

To the supreme controller who possesses an eternal form of blissful knowledge, whose glistening earrings swing to and fro, who brilliantly manifested Himself in Gokula, who stole the butter that the *gopīs* kept hanging from the rafters of their storerooms, and who then quickly jumped down from the mortar and ran in retreat in fear of Mother Yaśodā but was ultimately caught, to that

Supreme Lord, Śrī Dāmodara, I offer my humble obeisances.

(2) *rudantam*—crying; *muhuḥ*—continuously; *netra*—of eyes; *yugmam*—both; *mṛjantam*—rubbing; *kara*—hands; *ambhoja*—lotus like; *yugmena*—with both; *sa-ātaṅka*—with fear; *netram*—whose eyes; *muhuḥ*—repeatedly; *śvāsa*—(with) quick breathing; *kampa*—(and) trembling; *trirekha*—three lines; *aṅka*—marked with; *kaṇṭha*—(His) neck; *sthita*—situated; *graivam*—(His) necklace; *dāmodaram*—Lord Dāmodara; *bhakti*—by devotion; *baddham*—bound up.

Upon seeing His mother's whipping stick, He cried and rubbed His eyes again and again with His two lotus hands. His eyes were fearful and His breathing quick, and as Mother Yaśodā bound His belly with ropes, He shivered in fright and His pearl necklace, which was around His neck marked with three lines, shook. To this Supreme Lord, Śrī Dāmodara, who is bound with His devotee's love, I offer my humble obeisances.

(3) *iti*—thus; *īdṛk*—such; *sva-līlābhiḥ*—by His own pastimes; *ānanda-kuṇḍe*—in the ocean of transcendental bliss; *sva*—His own; *ghoṣam*—cowherd community; *nimajjantam*—plunging; *ākhyāpayantam*—revealing; *tadīya*—His; *īśita*—

sovereignty; *jñeṣu*—among those who know; *bhaktaiḥ*—by His devotees; *jitatvam*—(His) subjugation; *punaḥ*—again and again; *premataḥ*—with love; *taṁ*—unto Him; *śata-āvṛtti*—hundreds of times; *vande*—I offer my respectful obeisances.

Again let me offer my respectful obeisances unto the Supreme Personality. O my Lord, I offer my obeisances hundreds and thousands of times with all affection, because by Your personal pastimes You plunge the gopīs into an ocean of nectar. Appreciating Your opulence, devotees generally declare that You are always subjugated by their feelings. (Translation from the *Śrī Caitanya-caritāmṛta, Madhya-līlā*, Chapter 19, Verse 230.)

(4) *varam*—benediction; *deva*—O Lord; *mokṣaṁ*—liberation; *na*—not; *mokṣa avadhim*—Vaikuṇṭha; *vā*—or; *na ca*—nor; *anyam*—any other; *vṛṇe*—pray for; *aham*—I; *vara īśāt*—from the Lord of benedictions; *api*—even; *iha*—in this world; *idam*—this; *te*—Your; *vapuḥ*—body; *nātha*—O Lord; *gopāla-bālam*—as a cowherd boy; *sadā*—always; *me manasi*—in my heart and mind; *āvirāstām*—may appear; *kim*—what is the use? *anyaiḥ*—with others.

O Lord, although You are able to give all kinds of benedictions, I do not pray to You for impersonal liberation, nor eternal life in Vaikuṇṭha, nor any other boon in this world. My only prayer is that Your wonderful form as a cowherd boy may always appear in my heart and mind. What is the use of any other benediction?

(5) *idam*—this; *te*—Your; *mukha ambhojam*—lotus face; *atyanta-nīlaiḥ*—very blackish; *vṛtam*—encircled; *kuntalaiḥ*—by locks of curling hair; *snigdha raktaiḥ*—soft and reddish; *ca*—and; *gopyā*—by the *gopī* (Yaśodā); *muhuḥ*—again and again; *cumbitam*—kissed; *bimba-raktā-dharam*—lips that are red like the ripe *bimba* fruit; *me manasi*—in my heart and mind; *āvirāstām*—may (this vision) be manifest; *alam*—of no use; *lakṣa-lābhaiḥ*—millions of gains.

O Lord, Your lotus face is encircled by locks of soft black curling hair tinged with red, and Your beautiful lips are reddish like the ripe *bimba* fruit. Your beautiful face is being kissed again and again by Mother Yaśodā. Millions of opulences are of no use to me, but may this vision constantly remain in my heart.

(6) *namaḥ*—obeisances to You; *deva*—O Lord; *dāmodara*—O Dāmodara; *ananta*—O unlimited one; *viṣṇo*—O Lord Viṣṇu; *prasīda*—please be pleased; *prabho*—O master; *duḥkha*—(of) sorrows;

jālābdhi—(in) an ocean; *magnam*—drowned; *kṛpā*—(of) mercy; *dṛṣṭi*—of (Your) glance; *vṛṣṭyā*—by the shower; *ati-dīnam*—very fallen; *bata*—alas; *anugṛhāṇa*—(please) be merciful; *īśa*—O controller; *mām*—me; *ajñam*—foolish; *edhi*—please be; *akṣi*—(before my) eyes; *dṛśyaḥ*—visible.

O unlimited Viṣṇu! O master! O Lord Dāmodara! I offer my obeisances unto You. Be pleased upon me! I am drowning in an ocean of sorrows. Please shower Your glance of mercy upon me; uplift this poor ignorant fool, and become visible before my eyes.

(7) *kuverātmajau*—the two sons of Kuvera; *baddha-mūrtya*—while bound (to the mortar); *eva*—indeed; *yadvat*—just as; *tvayā*—by You; *mocitau*—where released; *bhakti-bhājau kṛtau*—where blessed with devotion; *ca*—and; *tathā*—in the same way; *prema-bhaktim*—pure devotional service; *svakām*—Your own; *me*—to me; *prayaccha*—please bestow; *na*—nor; *mokṣe*—in liberation; *grahaḥ*—seizing; *me*—my; *asti*—there is; *dāmodara*—O Dāmodara; *iha*—here.

O Lord Dāmodara, in Your form as a baby Mother Yaśodā bound You with a rope to a wooden grinding mortar. You then freed the sons of Kuvera, Maṇigrīva and Nalakūvara, who were cursed to stand as trees, and You gave them the chance to become Your devotees. In this same way, please give me Your own *prema-bhakti*. I have no desire for liberation into Your effulgence.

(8) *namaḥ*—obeisances; *te*—unto You; *astu*—let there be; *dāmne*—to the rope; *sphurat*—shining; *dīpti dhāmne*—the abode of effulgence; *tvadīya udarāya*—unto Your belly; *atha*—thus; *viśvasya*—of the universe; *dhāmne*—shelter; *namaḥ*—obeisances; *rādhikāyai*—unto Śrimatī Rādhārāṇī; *tvadīya priyāyai*—unto Your beloved; *namaḥ*—obeisances; *ananta-līlāya*—who manifests unlimited pastimes; *devāya*—unto the Supreme Lord; *tubhyam*—unto You.

I offer my obeisances to the shining rope that binds Your belly, and to Your belly, which is the abode of the entire universe. I humbly bow down to Your most beloved Śrīmatī Rādhārāṇī, and I offer all obeisances unto You, the Supreme Lord who displays unlimited pastimes.

Vaiṣṇava Practices

The Basic Philosophy of Kṛṣṇa Consciousness

The philosophy of the Hare Kṛṣṇa movement (a monotheistic tradition) is summarized in the following eight points by Śrīla Prabhupāda:

1. By sincerely cultivating the authentic spiritual science presented in the *Bhagavad-gītā* and other Vedic scriptures, we can become free from anxiety and achieve a state of pure, unending, blissful consciousness.

2. Each of us is not the material body but an eternal spirit soul, part and parcel of God (Kṛṣṇa). As such, we are all the eternal servants of Kṛṣṇa and are interrelated through Him, our common father.

3. Kṛṣṇa is the eternal, all-knowing, omnipresent, all-powerful, and all-attractive Personality of Godhead. He is the seed-giving father of all living beings and the sustaining energy of the universe. He is the source of all incarnations of God.

4. The *Vedas* are the oldest scriptures in the world. The essence of the *Vedas* is found in the *Bhagavad-gītā*, a literal record of Kṛṣṇa's words spoken five thousand years ago in India. The goal of Vedic knowledge—and of all religions—is to achieve love of God.

5. We can perfectly understand the knowledge of self-realization through the instructions of a genuine spiritual master—one who is free from selfish motives, who teaches the science of God explained in the *Bhagavad-gītā,* and whose mind is firmly fixed in meditation on Kṛṣṇa.

6. All that we eat should first be offered to Lord Kṛṣṇa with prayers. In this way Kṛṣṇa accepts the offering and blesses it for our purification.

7. Rather than living in a self-centered way we should act for the pleasure of Lord Kṛṣṇa. This is known as *bhakti-yoga,* the science of devotional service.

8. The most effective means for achieving God consciousness in this Age of Kali, or quarrel, is to chant the holy names of the Lord: Hare Kṛṣṇa, Hare Kṛṣṇa, Kṛṣṇa Kṛṣṇa, Hare Hare/ Hare Rāma, Hare Rāma, Rāma Rāma, Hare Hare.

Kṛṣṇa Consciousness at Home

In his books Śrīla Prabhupāda makes it clear how important it is for everyone to practice Kṛṣṇa consciousness, devotional service to Lord Kṛṣṇa. By following the teachings of Kṛṣṇa consciousness at home you can sanctify your home, making

Kṛṣṇa the center, and thus convert your home into a temple and *āśrama*.

Spiritual life, like material life, means practical activity. The difference is that whereas we perform material activities for the benefit of ourselves or those we consider ours, we perform spiritual activities for the satisfaction of Lord Kṛṣṇa, under the guidance of the scriptures and the spiritual master. The key is to accept the guidance of the scripture and the guru. Kṛṣṇa declares in the *Bhagavad-gītā* that a person can achieve neither happiness nor the supreme destination of life—going back to Godhead, back to Lord Kṛṣṇa—if he or she does not follow the injunctions of the scriptures. And *how* to follow the scriptural rules by engaging in practical service to the Lord—that is explained by a bona fide spiritual master. Without following the instructions of a spiritual master who is in an authorized chain of disciplic succession coming from Kṛṣṇa Himself, we cannot make spiritual progress. The practices outlined here are the timeless practices of *bhakti-yoga* as given by the foremost spiritual master and exponent of Kṛṣṇa consciousness in our time, His Divine Grace A.C. Bhaktivedanta Swami Prabhupāda, founder-*ācārya* of the International Society for Krishna Consciousness (ISKCON).

The purpose of spiritual knowledge is to bring us closer to God, or Kṛṣṇa. Kṛṣṇa says in the

Bhagavad-gītā (18.55), *bhaktyā māṁ abhijānāti:* "I can be known only by devotional service." Knowledge guides us in proper action. Spiritual knowledge directs us to satisfy the desires of Kṛṣṇa through practical engagements in His loving service. Without practical application, theoretical knowledge is of little value.

Spiritual knowledge is meant to direct us in all aspects of life. We should endeavor, therefore, to organize our lives in such a way as to follow Kṛṣṇa's teachings as far as possible. We should try to do our best, to do more than is simply convenient. Then it will be possible for us to rise to the transcendental plane of Kṛṣṇa consciousness, even while living far from a temple.

Chanting the Hare Kṛṣṇa Mantra

The first principle in devotional service is to chant the Hare Kṛṣṇa *mahā-mantra* (*mahā* means "great"; *mantra* means "sound that liberates the mind from ignorance"):

Hare Kṛṣṇa, Hare Kṛṣṇa, Kṛṣṇa Kṛṣṇa, Hare Hare
Hare Rāma, Hare Rāma, Rāma Rāma, Hare Hare

You can chant these holy names of the Lord anywhere and at any time, but it is best to set a specific time of day to regularly chant. The early morning hours are ideal.

The chanting can be done in two ways: singing the *mantra,* called *kīrtana* (usually done in a group), and saying the *mantra* to oneself, called *japa*. Concentrate on hearing the sound of the holy names. As you chant, pronounce the names clearly and distinctly, addressing Kṛṣṇa in a prayerful mood. When your mind wanders, bring it back to the sound of the Lord's names. Chanting is a prayer to Kṛṣṇa that means "O energy of the Lord [Hare], O all-attractive Lord [Kṛṣṇa], O Supreme Enjoyer [Rāma], please engage me in Your service." (For a further explanation please see page nine.) The more attentively and sincerely you chant these names of God, the more spiritual progress you will make.

Since God is all-powerful and all-merciful, He has kindly made it very easy for us to chant His names, and He has also invested all His powers in them. The names of God and God Himself are identical. This means that when we chant the holy names of Kṛṣṇa and Rāma we are directly associating with God and being purified. Therefore we should always try to chant with devotion and reverence. When a devotee chants Hare Kṛṣṇa,

Kṛṣṇa and His internal potency are dancing on the tongue of the devotee.

When you chant alone, it is best to chant on *japa* beads. This not only helps you fix your attention on the holy name, but it also helps you count the number of times you chant the *mantra* daily.

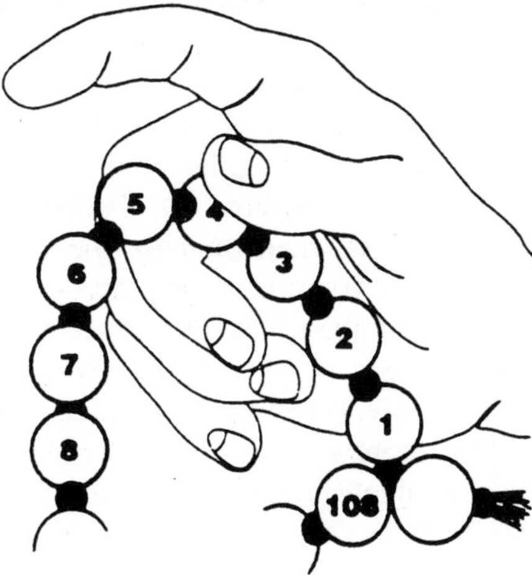

Each strand of *japa* beads consists of 108 small beads and one large bead, the head bead. Begin on a bead next to the head bead and gently roll it between the thumb and the middle finger of your right hand as you chant the full Hare Kṛṣṇa *mantra*, then move to the next bead and repeat the process. In this way, chant on each of the 108 beads until you reach the head bead again. This is one round of *japa.* Then, without chanting on the head bead, reverse the beads and start your second round on the last bead you chanted on. It generally takes from seven to eight minutes to chant one round for one who is practiced in chanting, although it may take longer in the beginning.

Initiated devotees vow before the spiritual master to chant at least sixteen rounds of the Hare Kṛṣṇa *mantra* daily. But even if you chant only one round a day, the principle is that once you commit yourself to chanting that round you should complete it every day without fail. When you feel you can chant more, then increase the minimum number of rounds you chant each day—but don't fall below that number. You can chant more than your fixed number, but you should maintain a set minimum each day. (Please note that the beads are sacred and therefore should never touch the ground or be put in an unclean place. To keep your beads clean, it's best to carry them in a special bead bag.)

Aside from chanting *japa,* you can also sing the Lord's holy names in *kīrtana*. While you can perform *kīrtana* individually, it is generally performed with others. A melodious *kīrtana* with family or friends is sure to enliven everyone. ISKCON devotees use traditional melodies and instruments, especially in the temple, but you can chant to any melody and use any musical instruments to accompany your chanting. As Lord Caitanya said, "There are no hard and fast rules for chanting Hare Kṛṣṇa."

Offenses to Be Avoided While Chanting Hare Kṛṣṇa

(From *The Nectar of Devotion*)

In order to derive the most benefit from chanting Hare Kṛṣṇa, and make the quickest advancement, one should avoid committing offenses while chanting.

The offenses against the chanting of the holy name are as follows: (1) To blaspheme the devotees who have dedicated their lives for propagating the holy name of the Lord. (2) To consider the names of demigods like Lord Śiva or Lord Brahmā to be equal to, or independent of, the name of Lord Viṣṇu. (3) To disobey the orders of the spiritual master. (4) To blaspheme the Vedic literature or literature in pursuance of the Vedic version. (5) To consider the glories of chanting Hare Kṛṣṇa to be imagination. (6) To give some interpretation on the holy name of the Lord. (7) To commit sinful activities on the strength of the holy name of the Lord. (8) To consider the chanting of Hare Kṛṣṇa one of the auspicious ritualistic activities offered in the *Vedas* as fruitive activities (*karma-kāṇḍa*). (9) To instruct a faithless person about the glories of the holy name. (10) To not have complete faith in the chanting of the holy names, and to maintain material attachments, even after understanding so many instructions on this matter.

It is also an offence to be inattentive while chanting the holy names.

Every devotee who claims to be a Vaiṣṇava must guard against these offenses in order to quickly achieve the desired success, Kṛṣṇa *prema.*

(Offenses 2, 7 and 9 are further explained in *The Nectar of Devotion* at the end of chapter eight.)

Marking the Body with Viṣṇu-Tilaka

Śrīla Prabhupāda glorifies *tilaka* in the following *Śrīmad-Bhāgavatam* purports:

> In Kali-yuga one can hardly acquire gold or jeweled ornaments, but the twelve *tilaka* marks on the body are sufficient as auspicious decorations to purify the body. [*Bhāg.* 4.12.28, purport]

> While decorating the body with *tilaka*, we give protection to the body by chanting twelve names of Viṣṇu. [*Bhāg.* 10.6.27-29, purport]

In the excerpts from the following letters, Śrīla Prabhupāda elaborates:

> So far as your dress is concerned, that is immaterial. But as a soldier you know that every soldier has got a uniform dress according to the army etiquette of regulation. Therefore, the army of Kṛṣṇa consciousness must have at least the *tilaka* on the forehead in all conditions. For your business you can wear your naval service uniform; similarly, if you have *tilaka* on your forehead as a soldier of Kṛṣṇa consciousness, you may not have so much objection, because it is essential. [letter from Śrīla Prabhupāda, 3 August 1969]

> All of you except a *sannyāsī* may dress yourself just like a fine up-to-date American gentleman, but one must have the *tilaka*, etc., as I have mentioned. [letter from Śrīla Prabhupāda, 11 October 1967]

The following quote is from *The Nectar of Devotion*:

> In the *Padma Purana* there is a statement describing how a Vaiṣṇava should decorate his body with *tilaka* and beads: "Persons who put *tulasī* beads on the neck, who mark twelve places of their bodies as Viṣṇu temples with Viṣṇu's symbolic representations, and who have *viṣṇu-tilaka* on their foreheads, are to be understood as the devotees of Lord Viṣṇu in this world. Their presence makes the world purified, and anywhere they remain, they make that place as good as Vaikuṇṭha."
>
> A similar statement is in the *Skanda Purāṇa*, which says, "Persons who are decorated with *tilaka* or *gopī-candana*, and who mark their bodies all over with the holy names of the Lord, and on whose necks and breasts there are *tulasī* beads, are never approached by the Yamadūtas." The Yamadūtas are the constables of King Yama (the lord of death), who punishes all sinful men. Vaiṣṇavas are never called for by such constables of Yamarāja. In the *Śrīmad-Bhāgavatam*, in the narration of Ajāmila's deliverance, it is said that Yamarāja gave clear intructions to his assistants not to approach the Vaiṣṇavas. Vaiṣṇavas are beyond the jurisdiction of Yamarāja's activities.

Tilaka refers to marks placed on the body using various substances, usually *gopī-candana.* The scriptures especially glorify *gopī-candana,* a special clay from Dvārakā. It is so pure that a cow-killer or any similarly sinful person can become free of sin simply by touching it. The *Padma Purāṇa* quotes Yamarāja as saying that *gopī-candana* and earth from the base of a *tulasī* plant are the best materials for making *tilaka.* Following in the footsteps of Lord Caitanya, one may also use mud from Rādhā-kuṇḍa in Vṛndāvana for making *tilaka. Candana* (sandalwood) that has been offered to the Deity may also be used as *tilaka.* If none of the above are available, one may apply *tilaka* using *caraṇāmṛta* water from the Deity; if *caraṇāmṛta* is unavailable, plain water may be used.

Preparing Tilaka

Tilaka is prepared by first placing one spoonful of water from an *ācamana* cup (about half a tea-spoon) into the palm of the left hand. Taking the piece of *tilaka* clay in the right hand, move it briskly in a clockwise direction in the left palm.

The following *mantras* from the *Uttara-khaṇḍa* of the *Padma Purāṇa* may be recited at this time.

You may optionally chant the Hare Kṛṣṇa *mahā-mantra* while preparing *tilaka.*

(1) *lalāṭe keśavaṁ dhyāyen*
nārāyaṇam athodare
vakṣaḥ-sthale mādhavaṁ tu
govindaṁ kaṇṭha-kūpake

(2) *viṣṇuṁ ca dakṣiṇe kukṣau*
bāhau ca madhusūdanam
trivikramaṁ kandhare tu
vāmanaṁ vāma-pārśvake

(3) *śrīdharaṁ vāma-bāhau tu*
hṛṣīkeśaṁ ca kandhare
pṛṣṭhe tu padma-nābhaṁ ca
kaṭyāṁ dāmodaraṁ nyaset

(4) *tat prakṣālana-toyaṁ tu*
vāsudeveti mūrdhani

WORD MEANINGS AND TRANSLATIONS

(1) *lalāṭe*—on the forehead; *keśavam*—Keśava (He who has fine hair); *dhyāyet*—one should meditate upon; *nārāyaṇam*—Nārāyaṇa; *atha*—then; *udare*—on the belly; *vakṣaḥ-stale*—on the chest; *mādhavam*—Mādhava (the husband of the goddess of fortune); *tu*—next; *govindam*—Govinda (He

who gives pleasure to the land, the cows and the senses); *kaṇṭha-kūpake*—on the hollow of the throat.

When one marks the forehead with *tilaka*, he should remember Keśava. When one marks the lower abdomen, he should remember Nārāyaṇa. For the chest, one should remember Mādhava, and when marking the hollow of the throat one should remember Govinda.

(2) *viṣṇum*—Viṣṇu; *ca*—and; *dakṣiṇe*—on the right side; *kukṣau*—on the belly; *bāhau*—on the arm; *ca*—and; *madhu-sūdanam*—Madhusūdana (the killer of the Madhu demon); *trivikramam*—Trivikrama (He who took three great steps, Lord Vāmana); *kandhare*—on the shoulder; *tu*—next; *vāmanam*—Vāmana (the dwarf incarnation); *vāma-pārśvake*—on the left side.

Lord Viṣṇu should be remembered when marking the right side of the belly, and Madhu-sūdana should be remembered when marking the right arm. Trivikrama should be remembered when marking the right shoulder, and Vāmana should be remembered when marking the left side of the belly.

(3) *śrīdharam*—Śrīdhara (He who embraces Lakṣmī); *vāma-bāhau*—on the left arm; *tu*—next; *hṛṣīkeśaṁ*—Hṛṣīkeśa (the Lord of the senses); *ca*—and; *kandhare*—on the shoulder; *pṛṣṭhe*—on the upper back; *tu*—next; *padma-nābham*—Padmanābha (He who has a lotus naval, or He from whose naval a lotus grows); *ca*—and; *kaṭyām*—on the lower back; *dāmodaram*—Dāmodara (He whose belly is bound with a rope); *nyaset*—one should place.

Śrīdhara should be remembered while marking the left arm, and Hṛṣīkeśa should be remembered when marking the left shoulder. Padmanābha and Dāmodara should be remembered when marking the upper and lower back.

(4) *tat*—that; *prakṣālana-toyam*—water from washing; *tu*—next; *vāsudeva*—Vāsudeva (the son of Vasudeva); *iti*—thus; *mūrdhani*—on the head.

Vāsudeva should be remembered when wiping the top of the back of the head with the water left after washing off the *tilaka*.

Applying Tilaka

After mixing the clay and water for a minute or two (as described at the bottom of page 95) the mixture of clay and water will be thick enough to apply (without running).

Using the ring finger of your right hand, make a mark pulling up from the root of the nose to the hairline. The little finger can now be used to make a clear space through the middle, which will form the two verticle lines. If crooked, these lines can also be straightened up using the little finger, provided it is free from clay. Next, make the leaf-shaped mark on the nose. This should extend from the first mark of two lines and come to a point not more than three-quarters of the length of the nose. Again it is made with the right ring finger and shaped with the little finger.

Now mark the other parts of the upper body. While marking the forehead and other places, names of Viṣṇu should be recited. Diagrams for doing this and the appropriate *mantras* are given on the following two pages.

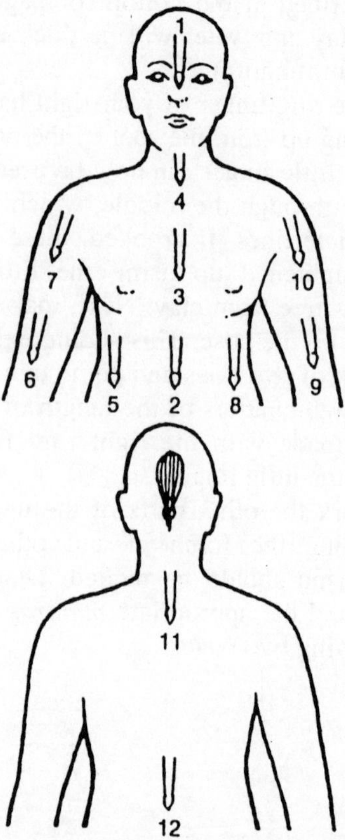
1
4
7
10
3
6
9
5
2
8
11
12

1. The forehead — *oṁ keśavāya namaḥ*
2. The belly — *oṁ nārāyaṇāya namaḥ*
3. The chest — *oṁ mādhavāya namaḥ*
4. The throat — *oṁ govindāya namaḥ*
5. The right side — *oṁ viṣṇave namaḥ*
6. The right arm — *oṁ madhusūdanāya namaḥ*
7. The right shoulder — *oṁ trivikramāya namaḥ*
8. The left side — *oṁ vāmanāya namaḥ*
9. The left arm — *oṁ śrīdharāya namaḥ*
10. The left shoulder — *oṁ hṛṣīkeśāya namaḥ*
11. The upper back — *oṁ padmanābhāya namaḥ*
12. The lower back — *oṁ dāmodarāya namaḥ*

If there is any clay left on the palm after applying *tilaka*, it can be returned to the piece of *tilaka*. After washing the hands wipe the water from the right hand on top of the back of the head and recite the following *mantra*:

oṁ vāsudevāya namaḥ

oṁ—address; *namaḥ*—I offer my humble obeisances.

I offer my humble obeisances unto the Supreme Personality of Godhead known as Keśava, Nārāyaṇa, Mādhava, Govinda, Viṣṇu, Madhusūdana, Trivikrama, Vāmana, Śrīdhara, Hṛṣīkeśa, Padmanābha, Dāmodara and Vāsudeva.

Setting Up an Altar in the Home

You will likely find that your *japa* and *kīrtana* are especially effective when done before an altar. Also the best place for offering food to Kṛṣṇa is on an altar. Lord Kṛṣṇa and His pure devotees are so kind that they allow us to worship them even through their pictures.

Setting up an altar at home means receiving the Lord and His pure devotees as your most honored guests. Where should you set up the altar? An ideal place would be clean, well lit, and free from drafts and household disturbances. A wall shelf, a mantelpiece, a corner table, or the top shelf of a bookcase will do. Some devotees build or have built a special altar with three steps, and some are able to keep a special room in their home, an altar room.

What do you need for an altar? Here are the essentials:

1. A picture of Śrīla Prabhupāda.
2. A picture of Lord Caitanya and His associates.
3. A picture of Śrī Śrī Rādhā and Kṛṣṇa.

You may also keep the following pictures on your altar:

4. A picture of Śrīla Bhaktisiddhānta, Śrīla Prabhupāda's spiritual master.
5. A picture of Śrīla Gaurakiśora dāsa Bābajī, Bhaktisiddhānta's spiritual master.
6. A picture of Śrīla Bhaktivinoda Ṭhākura, Gaurakiśora's spiritual master.
7. A picture of Śrīla Jagannātha dāsa Bābājī, Bhaktivinoda's spiritual master.
8. A picture of the six Gosvāmīs of Vṛndāvana.
9. A picture of Lord Nṛsiṁhadeva.

After one has been chanting sixteen rounds a day for at least six months, and after one has been formally accepted as an aspiring disciple by a spiritual master he/she may also put his/her spiritual master's picture on the altar.

In addition to the above pictures, you may want water cups (one for each picture), candles with holders or an oil lamp or lamps, a special plate and other utensils for offering food, a small bell, an *ācamana* cup and spoon, incense, an incense holder, and fresh flowers, which you may offer in vases or simply place before each picture.

If you have a three step altar, the picture of Rādhā and Kṛṣṇa should be on the top step, flanked by the picture of the Pañca-tattva on Their right and by the picture of Lord Nṛsiṁhadeva on Their left. On the middle step should be the pictures of the *gurus* in the following order from our left to right when facing them: initiating *guru,* Śrīla Prabhupāda, Bhaktisiddhānta, Gaurakiśora dāsa, Bhaktivinoda, Jagannātha dāsa and the six Gosvāmīs. You can also have a two step altar, mounting the pictures of Rādhā and Kṛṣṇa, the Pañca-tattva and Lord Nṛsiṁhadeva on the wall. The upper step will be used for the *gurus.* The bottom step of either type of altar is used for making offerings of food preparations. You can also have a two step altar with the *viṣṇu-tattva* pictures on the top step, the *guru-tattva* pictures on the bottom step, and with a small table placed in front for making offerings and another small table on the left for holding *ārati* paraphernalia. These are not the only ways to set up an altar, but are only given in order to give some guidance. Please consult with some senior devotee for further guidance.

Carefully clean the altar each morning. Cleanliness is essential in Deity worship. If you have water cups, rinse them out and fill them with fresh water daily. Then place them conveniently close to the pictures. You should remove flowers in vases as soon as they're slightly wilted, or daily if you've offered them at the base of the pictures. You should offer fresh incense at least once a day, and, if possible, light candles or an oil lamp and place them/it near the pictures when you're chanting near the altar.

Prasādam: How to Eat Spiritually

By His immense transcendental energies, Kṛṣṇa can actually convert matter into spirit. If we place an iron rod in a fire, before long the rod becomes red hot and acts just like fire. In the same way, food prepared for and offered to Kṛṣṇa with love and devotion becomes completely spiritualized. Such food is called Kṛṣṇa *prasādam*, which means "the mercy of Lord Kṛṣṇa."

Eating *prasādam* is a fundamental practice of *bhakti-yoga*. In other forms of yoga one must artificially repress the senses, but the *bhakti-yogī* can engage his or her senses in a variety of pleasing spiritual activities, such as tasting delicious food offered to Lord Kṛṣṇa. In this way the senses gradually become spiritualized and bring the devotee more and more transcendental pleasure by being engaged in devotional service. Such spiritual pleasure far surpasses any material experience.

In the *Caitanya-caritāmṛta, Antya-līlā*, chapter sixteen, verses 109 to 112, Lord Caitanya said of *prasādam*, "Everyone has tasted these foods before. However, now that they have been prepared for Kṛṣṇa and offered to Him with devotion, these foods have acquired extraordinary tastes and uncommon fragrances. Just taste them and see the difference in the experience! Apart from the taste, even the fragrance pleases the mind and makes one forget any other fragrance. Therefore, it should be understood that the spiritual nectar of Kṛṣṇa's lips must have touched these ordinary foods and imparted to them all their transcendental qualities."

Eating food offered to Kṛṣṇa is the perfection of vegetarianism. In itself, being a vegetarian is not enough; after all, even the pigeons and monkeys are vegetarians. But when we go beyond vegetarianism to a diet of *prasādam*, our eating becomes helpful in achieving the goal of human life—reawakening the soul's original relationship with God. In the *Bhagavad-gītā* (3.13) Lord Kṛṣṇa says that unless one eats only food that has been offered to Him in sacrifice, one will suffer the reactions of *karma.*

"Food offered to Lord Viṣṇu and then taken by us makes us sufficiently resistant to material affection, and one who is accustomed to this practice is called a devotee of the Lord. Therefore, a person in Kṛṣṇa consciousness, who eats only food offered to Kṛṣṇa, can counteract all reactions of past material infections, which are impediments to the progress of self-realization. On the other hand, one who does not do so continues to increase the volume of sinful action, and this prepares the next body to resemble hogs and dogs, to suffer the resultant reactions of all sins. The material world is full of contaminations, and one who is immunized by accepting *prasādam* of the Lord (food offered to Viṣṇu) is saved from the attack, whereas one who does not do so becomes subjected to contamination."

—*Bhagavad-gītā As It Is,* 3.14, purport

Preparing Food for Offering to Kṛṣṇa

When you are selecting the foods you will offer to Kṛṣṇa, you need to know what is offerable and what is not. In the *Bhagavad-gītā* (9.26) Lord Kṛṣṇa states, "If one offers Me with love and devotion a leaf, a flower, a fruit, or water, I will accept it." From this verse it is understood that we can offer Kṛṣṇa foods prepared from milk products, vegetables, fruits, nuts and grains. Meat, fish and eggs are not offerable. Garlic and onions, although vegetarian, are also forbidden. They are in the modes of ignorance and passion. They therefore tend to agitate the mind, making meditation difficult. (*Hing,* or asafoetida, is a tasty substitute for them in cooking, and is available at many Indian grocery shops.) Nor can you offer to Kṛṣṇa coffee or tea that contain caffeine. If you like these beverages, purchase caffeine-free coffee, Chikree and herbal teas like Rooibos.

While shopping, be aware that you may find meat, fish and egg products mixed with other foods; so be sure to read labels carefully. For instance, the term "stabilizer" may be vegetarian or it may be gelatin, a substance made from the horns, hooves and bones of slaughtered animals. "Albumen" comes from egg whites. Also, make sure the cheese you buy contains no animal (veal) rennet, an enzyme extracted from the stomach tissues of slaughtered calves. "Microbial rennet" is all right. Kosher cheeses (marked with a diamond with the letters B and D inside it) do not contain animal rennet.

Also avoid foods cooked by nondevotees. According to the subtle laws of nature, the cook acts upon the food not only physically but mentally as well. Food thus becomes an agent for subtle influences on your consciousness. The state of mind of the cook influences the cooked preparations. So if you eat food cooked by nondevotees—employees working in a factory, for example—then you're sure to absorb a dose of materialism and *karma.* As far as possible use only fresh, natural ingredients.

In preparing food, cleanliness is the most important principle. Nothing impure should be offered to Kṛṣṇa; so keep your kitchen very clean. Always wash your hands thoroughly before entering the kitchen. While preparing food, do not taste it, for you are cooking the meal not for yourself but for the pleasure of Kṛṣṇa.

Performing Ācamana

Ācamana, or sipping water, is a means of purification. As immersing the body in water brings about physical and subtle cleansing, so taking water infused with *mantras* into the body by sipping water performs a similar function. Thus where purification is required but it is inconvenient to bathe, *ācamana* is prescribed. *Ācamana* is performed before offering food, before offering *ārati*, before reciting *mantras*, before making vows etc.

To perform *ācamana* sit cross-legged on an *āsana* (sitting mat), preferably made of *kuśa* grass, silk or wool. If you are performing *ācamana* before offering *ārati* you may stand while performing it.

With a small spoon take some water from an *ācamana* cup and clean both hands by sprinkling them with water. Holding the *ācamana* spoon in your left hand, put a few drops of water into the right palm. While looking at the water chant the *mantra*:

oṁ keśavāya namaḥ

and then silently sip the water from the base of the right palm. Again put a few drops of water into the right palm. While looking at the water chant the *mantra*:

oṁ nārāyaṇāya namaḥ

and sip the water from the base of the right palm. Again put a few drops of water into the right palm. While looking at the water chant the *mantra*:

oṁ mādhavāya namaḥ

and sip the water from the base of the right palm. Clean your right hand (from having been touched by your lips) with a few drops of water from the *ācamana* cup, throwing the water aside.

Offering Food to Kṛṣṇa

Keep a plate, a spoon, a tumbler and several small bowls solely for offering food to Kṛṣṇa. They should not have been previously used for eating by anyone else and should not be used for any other purpose. Stainless steel utensils are quite acceptable for home worship. If you have the means, silver, or silver-plated utensils are better. If it is available, banana leaf is considered the best.

1. On the plate and in the tumbler and bowls, nicely arrange the food preparations for offering. Perform *ācamana* and offer obeisances to your spiritual master. (Until you are formally accepted by an initiating spiritual master, you should offer obeisances to Śrīla Prabhupāda.) Set the offering plate on the altar, or on a small table before the altar.

2. With your right hand purify the *bhoga* (unoffered food) by lightly sprinkling it with water from an *ācamana* cup while chanting the *mahā-mantra.*

3. Sitting on an *āsana* (sitting mat) reserved solely for worshipping purposes, before the altar, and while ringing a bell, recite three times the

praṇāma prayer(s) to your spiritual master, begging permission to assist him in his service to the Lord. Until formally accepted by an initiating spiritual master recite the following *praṇāma* prayers to Śrīla Prabhupāda three times:

nama oṁ viṣṇu-pādāya kṛṣṇa-preṣṭhāya bhū-tale
śrīmate bhaktivedānta-svāmin iti nāmine

namaste sārasvate deve gaura-vāṇī-pracāriṇe
nirviśeṣa-śūnyavādī-pāścātya-deśa-tāriṇe

(Translations and word meanings for these prayers are found in the beginning of this book.)

Chant the following prayer to Lord Caitanya three times, requesting His mercy:

namo mahā-vadānyāya kṛṣṇa-prema-pradāya te
kṛṣṇāya kṛṣṇa-caitanya-nāmne gaura-tviṣe namaḥ

Chant the following prayer three times, offering respects to Lord Kṛṣṇa:

namo brahmaṇya-devāya go-brāhmaṇa-hitāya ca
jagad-dhitāya kṛṣṇāya govindāya namo namaḥ

4. After offering the food to the Lord, wait at least five or ten minutes (according to the size of the offering) for Him to partake of the preparations. At this time you may chant the Hare Kṛṣṇa *mantra* and/or other Vaiṣṇava songs.

5. Clap your hands three times and remove the plate, praying that you have served the the Lord and His associates to Their full satisfaction.

Then you should transfer the *prasādam* from the Lord's eating utensils and wash them.

The above procedure is a "proper" standard for home worship. Sometimes, such as when traveling, etc., the food offerings may simply be placed in front of some pictures and the prayers recited according to the circumstances. When there are no pictures available, or in awkward circumstances, one may recite the prayers and mentally remember the Lord and His associates in order to offer food. It is always better to follow the higher standard whenever possible though.

Offering Ārati

Please note: There are different spellings. **Ārati** is Bengali. **Āratī** is Hindi. The Sanskrit term is **ārātrika**.

"If someone sees the face of the Lord while *ārati* is going on, he can be relieved of all sinful reactions coming from many, many thousands and millions of years past. He is even excused from the killing of a *brāhmaṇa* or similar prohibited activities."

—*Skanda Purāṇa*

There are basically two types of *ārati*, the full *ārati* and the *dhūpa ārati*. For a full *ārati* the following items are offered: incense sticks *(dhūpa, agar-battī)*, a camphor lamp (for midday *ārati*), a ghee lamp with an odd number of wicks (at least five), a conch with *arghya* (water), a handkerchief, flowers on a plate, a *cāmara* (yak-tail whisk), and a peacock fan (only in warm weather). For a *dhūpa ārati* the following items are offered: incense sticks, flowers on a plate, a *cāmara*, and a peacock fan (only in warm weather). For *Tulasī ārati* incense sticks, a ghee lamp with an odd number of wicks (at least one), and flowers on a plate are offered.

Required Paraphernalia

- Make sure the following items are present:

  For all *āratis*:

  1) a bell;
  2) an *ācamana* cup containing water and a spoon;
  3) matches or a lighter, and (optionally) an oil or ghee lamp for lighting incense and *ārati* lamps.

  In addition, for *āratis* except for *Tulasī ārati*:

  1) a conch (for blowing) with a water-filled *loṭā* for purifying it;
  2) a receptacle for catching the water from rinsing the conch.

  In addition, for full *āratis*:

  1) an incense holder with an odd number of incense sticks;
  2) a ghee lamp with an odd number of wicks (at least five);
  3) a conch for offering water, with a stand;
  4) a container for the water which is to be offered;
  5) a small throw-out container for the offered water (may be a sprinkler with the top removed);

6) a handkerchief;
7) fragrant flower(s) on a plate;
8) a *cāmara* (yak-tail whisk);
9) a peacock fan (only in warm weather).

For *dhūpa-āratis*:

1) an incense holder with an odd nmber of sticks;
2) fragrant flower(s) on a plate;
3) a *cāmara*;
4) a peacock fan (only in warm weather).

Preliminary Activities for Ārati

- Perform *ācamana*.
- Offer obeisances to your spiritual master, requesting to assist him in the worship.
- You may now light an oil or ghee lamp for lighting incense and the *ārati* lamp.
- Blow the conch three times and rinse it over the receptacle for that purpose.
- Wash your hands with water from the *ācamana* cup.
- During the *ārati* ceremony, devotees should perform *kīrtana* before the altar. If there is no one to chant, the *pūjārī* performing the *ārati* may either sing or play a recording of a *kīrtana*.

Purifying the Items to be Offered

Before offering each item of worship, purify both your right hand and the item by sprinkling them with water from the *ācamana* cup. You can purify the item in either of two ways: 1) place a few drops of water in your right hand and then sprinkle it lightly over the item with a single motion of your hand, so that the water comes off your fingertips; or 2) take the spoon in your right hand and sprinkle water on the item directly from the spoon.

Procedure for Offering the Items

- While standing on an *āsana* (See page 109.) and ringing a bell with your left hand, with your right hand first present the lit incense to your spiritual master or to Śrīla Prabhupāda (See page 103, paragraph one.), and pray, "My dear Guru Mahārāja, and/or my dear Śrīla Prabhupāda, please allow me to assist you in the worship of the Lord and His associates."

  Āratī paraphernalia should be offered gracefully, in a meditative mood. Do not be either to slow or too fast, and do not perform it in a showy manner, but as a humble servant of your spiritual master and the assembled Vaiṣṇavas. Stand to the left of the altar (as viewed from the temple room).

Along with the worship of one's own spiritual master, devotees in ISKCON worship His Divine Grace A.C. Bhaktivedanta Swami Prabhupāda as both the Founder-Ācārya of ISKCON and as the *śikṣa-guru* for all devotees in ISKCON. One should honor him when performing *ārati* by presenting the *ārati* items to Śrīla Prabhupāda after presenting them to one's own spiritual master.

- Then, with the consciousness that you are offering it on behalf of your spiritual master and Śrīla Prabhupāda, offer the incense with the full number of circles (listed below) to the main Deity.

- After offering the incense to the main Deity, offer it as *prasāda* to the Lord's associates in descending order, and to the *guru-paramparā* —senior to junior. (For example: Kṛṣṇa, Rādhārāṇī, Caitanya Mahāprabhu, Lord Nṛsiṁhadeva, Tulasī Devī, Jagannātha dāsa, Bhaktivinoda, Gaurakiśora, Bhaktisiddhānta, Śrīla Prabhupāda, and finally one's initiating guru. This may vary according to the Deities or pictures on the altar.) This may be done with seven or three circles for each personality, depending on time allowance.

- Then offer it (with one or three circles) to the assembled Vaiṣṇavas as the *prasāda* of the Lord and His associates.

- Offer the remaining items in a similar way. When offering each item, say softly to each personality, "Please accept this offering of [incense, lamps, etc.]."

- Offered items should not be mixed with unoffered items. You may place offered items back on the plate that was used to bring in the paraphernalia, provided no unoffered paraphernalia remains on it.

How to Offer Each Item

Offer all items, except the *cāmara* and fan, by moving them in clockwise circles while ringing a bell with your left hand (above waist level), fixing your attention on the Deities.

- **Incense:** Offer seven circles around the whole body of the worshipped person. (Incense, water in a conch, handkerchief and flowers can be offered with fewer circles if time is short. The main item of the *ārati* ceremony is the lamp, for which *śāstra* gives specific numbers of circles. In general, the exact number of circles for offering a given item is not considered critical.)

- **Lamp**(s): Offer four circles to the lotus feet, two circles to the navel, and three circles to the person's face; then offer seven circles to the person's whole body.
- **Water in a conch (*Arghya*):** Offer three circles to the person's head and seven circles to whole body. Then pour a small amount of the offered water into the throw-out container before proceeding to offer the *arghya* to the next personality.
- **Handkerchief:** Offer seven times around the person's body.
- **Flowers:** Offer seven times around the person's body.
- ***Cāmara*:** Wave before the Lord and/or His associates a suitable number of times.
- **Peacock Fan:** Wave before the Lord and/or His associates a suitable number of times.

You may distribute the lamp(s), *arghya* water and flowers to the assembled devotees (generally in order of seniority) immediately after offering them. (Women who are having their monthly period should not touch the lamp.)

Completing the Āratī

- After completing the *ārati,* blow the conch three times as at the beginning of the *ārati.*
- Chant the *prema-dhvani mantras* (page 36) if the *kīrtana* leader or another devotee present does not chant them.
- Then with joined palms offer *praṇāma* prayers softly to your spiritual master and Their Lordships.
- Remove the *ārati* paraphernalia from the altar, clean the area and articles and offer *daṇḍavat-praṇāmas* (prostrated obeisances).

Please note: The preceding sections, Performing Ācamana, Offering Food to Kṛṣṇa, and Offering Āratī, are based on the procedures described in *Pañcarātra-Pradīpa* compiled by the GBC Deity Worship Research Group and have been somewhat simplified for congregational practice. More elaborate procedures which are found in the above mentioned book may be in use for the Deity worship in the temple.

Worshipping Tulasī Devī

"Tulasī Devī is a pure devotee of Kṛṣṇa, and she should be treated with the same respect given to all of Kṛṣṇa's pure devotees. Simply by worshipping her faithfully, a devotee can get himself free from all material miseries. In *The Nectar of Devotion* I have given two verses from the *Skanda Purāṇa*, one of which is, '*Tulasī* is auspicious in all respects. Simply by seeing, simply by touching, simply by remembering, simply by praying to, simply by bowing before, simply by hearing about or simply by sowing this tree, there is always auspiciousness. Anyone who comes in touch with the *tulasī* tree in the above-mentioned ways lives eternally in the Vaikuṇṭha world.'

"So from this verse we can understand how pure the service is which Tulasī offers to Śrī Kṛṣṇa. So we should also endeavor to become the servant of Tulasī Devī. . . .Tulasī Devī never goes back to Godhead; she is always with Godhead. She is a pure devotee and thus she has appeared on this planet to render service to Kṛṣṇa by being offered at His lotus feet in all temples throughout the world."

—Letter from Śrīla Prabhupāda
to Rādhāvallabha Dās

All parts of Tulasī Devī, her leaves, her flowers, her wood, her shade, and even the soil around her roots, are auspicious and worshipable. Because of this devotees of Kṛṣṇa wear strings of beads made of Tulasī wood around their necks at all times, signifying their devotion to Lord Kṛṣṇa and also deriving great benefit for themselves.

Śrīmatī Tulasī Devī is an expansion of Śrimatī Vṛndā Devī, the Vṛndāvana *gopī* in charge of arranging the details of Rādhā and Kṛṣṇa's *līlā*. By her mercy, Vṛndā Devī has appeared in this material world as the plant Tulasī Devī, giving us a chance to serve her and to beg her to bestow upon us her greatest boon—love of Kṛṣṇa and the privilege of devotional service to Him.

The Formal Worship of Śrīmatī Tulasī Devī

Śrīla Prabhupāda has outlined a formal worship program for Tulasī Devī that is standard in all ISKCON temples. This same program may also be observed in the home. This worship begins with the offering of obeisances to Tulasī and chanting the *Tulasī Praṇāma Mantra* (Page 20) three times. Then an *ārati* is offered with incense sticks, a ghee lamp with an odd number of wicks (at least one), and fragrant flowers on a plate. During the *ārati* the *Tulasī Kīrtana* (Page 21) is sung. After the *ārati*, Tulasī is then circumambulated (at least three times) while the *Tulasī Pradakṣiṇa Mantra* (Page 23) and (optionally) Hare Kṛṣṇa are chanted. During or after the circumambulation each devotee waters Tulasī. She is again offered obeisances to with the chanting of her *praṇāma mantra* three times. The English translation of the *Tulasī Kīrtana* may be recited at the end if so desired.

Collecting Leaves and Mañjarīs

Tulasī Devī is blessed with the benediction of always being present on the Lord's lotus feet and on all presentations offered to Him. Tulasī can be offered only to Kṛṣṇa and His *viṣṇu-tattva* expansions, never to anyone else. While collecting leaves and *mañjarīs* (flowers) for this purpose, chant this mantra:

tulasy amṛta-janmāsi
sadā tvaṁ keśava-priyā
keśavārthaṁ cinomi tvaṁ
varadā bhava śobhane

tulasi—O Tulasī; *amṛta-janmāsi*—(O you who are) born from nectar; *sadā*—always; *tvam*—you; *keśava-priyā*—(O you who are) dear to Lord Keśava; *keśava-artham*—for Lord Keśava; *cinomi*—I collect; *tvam*—you; *varadā*—a giver of benedictions; *bhava*—(please) become; *śobhane*—O most beautiful one.

"O Tulasī Devī, your birth is from nectar, and you are always dear to Lord Keśava. It is for Lord Keśava that I collect your leaves and *mañjarīs*. O most beautiful Tulasī, please give us the boon of service to the Lord."

Gauḍiya Vaiṣṇavas refrain from collecting Tulasī leaves and *mañjarīs* on Dvādaśī day (the day after Ekādaśī).

Observing Ekādaśī

In the *Bhakti-rasāmṛta-sindhu (The Nectar of Devotion)* Śrīla Rūpa Gosvāmī mentions observing fasting on Ekādaśī day as one of the basic priciples to be followed by Vaiṣṇavas. In the *Brahma-vaivarta Purāṇa* it is said that one who observes fasting on Ekādaśī day is released from all kinds of sinful activities and advances in pious life.

Ekādaśī comes twice a month on the eleventh day of the moon, both waning and waxing. ("Ekādaśī" means "eleventh day.") The specific dates for Ekādaśī are given on the Vaiṣṇava calendar. The devotees observe Ekādāśī by fasting from grains (wheat, rice, maize, oats, barley etc.) and pulses (beans, peas and *dāl*). In the *Padma Purāṇa* it is described that Pāpa-puruṣa (sin personified) was given permission to take shelter of grains on Ekādaśī. In the *Śrī Caitanya-caritāmṛta* (Adi 15.9) we read how Lord Caitanya established the principle of fasting on Ekādaśī by falling at the feet of His mother and requesting her to give Him one thing in charity, "My dear mother, please do not eat grains on Ekādaśī day."

One may use spices on Ekādśī, although mustard seeds should be avoided. (Many commercially ground spices are mixed with flour, so it is best to either use whole spices or grind your own for Ekādaśī.) You should not use powdered asafoetida (*hing*), since it is compounded with wheat flour. Sesame seeds are also to be avoided, except on Ṣaṭ-ṭilā Ekādaśī when they may be offered and eaten. (This Ekādaśī appears about eleven days before the appearance day of Advaita Ācārya, usually in January.) Margarine may be made from grain products such as maize oil or soya lecithin (an emulsifier). Use butter instead of margarine on Ekādaśī.

There is also a specific time period on the morning after Ekādaśī in which to break the fast by eating grains. The times for this period vary from region to region and can be obtained from your local temple.

The basic principle is not just to fast, but to minimize the demands of the body and to engage our time in the service of the Lord by chanting or performing similar services. The best thing to do on fasting days is to remember the pastimes of Govinda and to hear and chant His holy names constantly.

Drinking Caraṇāmṛta

(From *The Nectar of Devotion*)

Caraṇāmṛta is obtained in the morning while the Lord is being bathed before dressing. Scented with perfumes and flowers, the water comes gliding down through his lotus feet and is collected and mixed with yoghurt. In this way this *caraṇāmṛta* not only becomes very tastefully flavored, but also has tremendous spiritual value. As described in the *Padma Purāṇa*, even a person who has never been able to give in charity, who has never been able to perform a great sacrifice, who has never been able to study the Vedas, who has never been able to worship the Lord—or, in other words, even one who has never done any pious activities—will become eligible to enter into the kingdom of God if he simply drinks the *caraṇāmṛta* which is kept in the temple. In the temple it is the custom that the *caraṇāmṛta* be kept in a large bowl. The devotees who come to visit and offer respect to the Deity take three drops of *caraṇāmṛta* very submissively and feel themselves happy in transcendental bliss.

Circumambulating the Deities or Temple of Viṣṇu

(From *The Nectar of Devotion*)

It is said in the *Hari-bhakti-sudhodaya*, "A person who is circumambulating the Deity of Viṣṇu can counteract the circumambulation of repeated birth and death in this material world." The conditioned soul is circumambulating through repeated births and deaths on account of his material existence, and this can be counteracted simply by circumambulating the Deity in the temple.

The Cāturmāsya ceremony is observed during the four months of the rainy season in India (approximately July, August, September and October), beginning from the month of Śrāvaṇa. During these four months, saintly persons who are accustomed to travel from one place to another to propagate Kṛṣṇa consciousness remain at one place, usually a holy place of pilgrimage. During these times, there are certain special rules and regulations which are strictly followed. It is stated in the *Skanda Purāṇa* that during this period, if someone circumambulates the temple of Viṣṇu at least four times, it is understood that he has travelled all over the universe. By such circumambulation, one is understood to have seen all the holy places where the Ganges water is flowing, and by following the regulative principles of Cāturmāsya one can very quickly be raised to the platform of devotional service.

Everyday Life: The Four Regulative Principles

Anyone serious about progressing in Kṛṣṇa consciousness must try to avoid the following four sinful activities:

1. Eating meat, fish or eggs. These foods are saturated with the modes of passion and ignorance and therefore cannot be offered to the Lord. A person who eats these foods participates in a conspiracy of violence against helpless animals and thus stops his spiritual progress dead in its tracks.

2. Gambling. Gambling invariably puts one into anxiety and fuels greed, envy and anger.

3. The use of intoxicants. Drugs, alcohol and tobacco, as well as any drinks or foods containing caffeine, cloud the mind, overstimulate the senses,

and make it impossible to understand or follow the principles of *bhakti-yoga.*

4. Illicit sex. This is sex outside of marriage or sex in marriage for any purpose other than procreation. Sex for pleasure compels one to identify with the body and takes one far from Kṛṣṇa consciousness. The scriptures teach that sex is the most powerful force binding us to the material world. Anyone serious about advancing in Kṛṣṇa consciousness should minimize sex or eliminate it entirely.

The Daily Temple Program

Maṅgal (full) Āratī	4:30 a.m.
Prayers to Lord Nṛsiṁhadeva	4:55
Tulasī Pūjā	5:00
Chanting Japa	5:15
Greeting the Deities	7:00
Śrīla Prabhupāda's Guru Pūjā	7:10
Śrīmad-Bhāgavatam Class	7:40
Dhūpa Āratī	8:00
Mid-day (full) Ārati	12:30 p.m.
Altar Closed	1:00 to 4:15
Afternoon Dhūpa Ārati	4:15
Sandhya (full) Ārati	7:00
Śayana (dhūpa) Ārati	8:30
Temple Closes	8:45

Temple and Vaiṣṇava Etiquette

1. One should remove ones shoes before entering the temple room.
2. One should wear clean attire and clean socks, and have clean feet when visiting the temple.
3. One should not to wear leather (belts, jackets, handbags, etc.) in the temple. Actually, one should completely avoid the use of leather. Śrīla Prabhupāda said, "Leather means violence." (*Śrīla Prabhupāda-līlāmṛta,* Vol. 3, p. 150)
4. After passing stool, one should bathe before coming before the Deities.
5. After eating one should rinse one's mouth and wash one's hands, and, if possible, one's feet before coming before the Deities.
6. One should offer obeisances with the left ṣide to the Deities as well as to the spiritual master, and never with one's feet towards the Deities or towards the spiritual master.
7. One should not be intoxicated when coming to the temple.
8. One should not cause a disturbance by arguing, raising one's voice, or passing air in the temple room.
9. One should avoid speaking unnecessarily about nondevotionl topics before the Deities.

10. One should not step over or touch one's feet to sacred paraphernalia such as *prasādam,* scriptures, sacred pictures, devotees, etc.
11. Cell phones should be switched off before entering the temple.
12. One should not take sacred things such as chanting beads, sacred pictures (including those on T-shirts), scripture, *hari-nāma cādars, prasādam,* etc. into the toilet.
13. One should not allow sacred things, such as those mentioned above, to touch the floor.
14. One should be very respectful towards other devotees.
15. One should bring some gift for the Deities, such as fruit, flowers, money, etc.

For further guidance in these matters one can read *The Nectar of Devotion,* chapters six and eight.

Sanskrit and Bengali Pronunciation Guide

The system of tranliteration used in this book conforms to a system that scholars have accepted to indicate the pronunciation of each sound in Sanskrit, Bengali and other Indian languages.

The short vowel **a** is pronounced like the **a** in **organ**, long **ā** like the **a** in **far**. In Bengali **a** is sometimes pronounced like **o**. Also in Bengali, final **a** is often silent. Short **i** is pronounced as in **pin**, long **ī** as in **pique**, short **u** as in **pull**, and long **ū** as in **rule**. The vowel **ṛ** is pronounced like the **ri** in **rim**, **e** like the **ey** in **they**, **o** like the **o** in **go**, **ai** like the **ai** in **aisle**, and **au** like the **ow** in **how**. The *anusvāra* (**ṁ**) is pronounced like the **n** in the French word *bo***n**. *Visarga* (**ḥ**) is pronounced as a final **h** sound. At the end of the second and fourth lines of a verse, **aḥ** is pronounced **aha**, **iḥ** is pronounced **ihi**, **uḥ** is pronounced **uhu**, **eḥ** is pronounced **ehi**, and **oḥ** is pronounced **ohu**.

The gutteral consonants—**k, kh, g, gh,** and **ṅ**—are pronounced from the throat in much the same way as in English. **K** is pronounced as in **kite**, **kh** as in **Eckhart**, **g** as in **give**, **gh** as in **dig-hard**, and **ṅ** as in **sing**.

The palatal consonants—**c, ch, j, jh,** and **ñ** are pronounced with the tongue touching the firm ridge behind the teeth. **C** is pronounced as in **chair**, **ch** as in **staunch-heart**, **j** as in **joy**, **jh** as in **hedgehog**, and **ñ** as in **canyon**. The combination **jñ** is an exception and is pronounced as **gy** (with a hard **g**). For example **jñāna** is pronounced **gyāna**.

The cerebral consonants—**ṭ, ṭh, ḍ, ḍh,** and **ṇ**—are pronounced with the tip of the tongue turned up and drawn back against the dome of the palate. **Ṭ** is pronounced as in **tub**, **ṭh** as in **light-heart**, **ḍ** as in **dove**, **ḍh** as in **red-hot**, and **ṇ** as in **nut**. The dental consonants—**t, th, d, dh,** and **n**—are pronounced in the same manner as the cerebrals, but with the forepart of the tongue against the teeth.

The labial consonants—**p, ph, b, bh,** and **m**—are pronounced with the lips. **P** is pronounced as in **pine**, **ph** as in **uphill**, **b** as in **bird**, **bh** as in **rub-hard**, and **m** as in **mother**. In Bengali **ph** is pronounced like **f**.

The semivowels—**y, r, l,** and **v**—are pronounced as in **yes**, **run**, **light**, and **vine** respectively. When **v** immediately follows a consonant it is pronounced like a **w**. For example **svāmī** is pronounced **swāmī**, **aśva** is pronounced **aśwa**, **dvāra** is pronounced **dwāra**. In Bengali **y** is often pronounced like the **j** in **jaw**.

The sibilants—ś and ṣ—are pronounced as the **sh** in **shine**, s as in sun. In Bengali **s** is often also pronounced like **sh**. The letter **h** is pronounced as in **home**.

These notes serve as guidelines for pronunciation, but, as with all languages, it is best to learn pronunciation by listening to an educated speaker of the respective language.